SOCIAL POLICY

Politics

Editor
PROFESSOR W. A. ROBSON
B.Sc (Econ), Ph.D, LL.M
*Professor Emeritus of Public Administration
in the University of London*

Social Policy

T. H. MARSHALL

*Professor Emeritus of Sociology
in the University of London*

HUTCHINSON UNIVERSITY LIBRARY
LONDON

HUTCHINSON & CO. (*Publishers*) LTD
178–202 Great Portland Street, London W.1

London Melbourne Sydney
Auckland Bombay Toronto
Johannesburg New York

★

First published 1965

© T. H. Marshall 1965

*This book has been set in Times New Roman,
printed in Great Britain on Smooth Wove paper
by The Anchor Press, Ltd., and bound by Wm.
Brendon & Son Ltd., both of Tiptree, Essex.*

Contents

Preface

'Social policy' is not a technical term with an exact meaning. In this book it is taken to refer to the policy of governments with regard to action having a direct impact on the welfare of the citizens, by providing them with services or income. The central core consists, therefore, of social insurance, public (or national) assistance, the health and welfare services, and housing policy. Education obviously belongs, but is omitted because it is the subject of another book in this series. So also is the treatment of crime, which figures here only in the form of a brief passage on juvenile delinquency. The book is divided into two parts. Part One traces the history from the last decades of the nineteenth century to about 1950; and Part Two surveys social policy in the early 1960's. Although the main emphasis is on the British story, an attempt has been made, especially in Part Two, to indicate the outlines of the situation in the more advanced countries of the contemporary world.

As this book is based not on original research but on secondary authorities and official publications, my debt to those who have worked in this field is enormous and obvious. I am particularly grateful to my former colleagues at the London School of Economics, most of whom are now members of the remarkable team headed by Professor Titmuss, for what I learned from working with them and for the response I received from the enquiries I addressed to some of them—from Dame Eileen Younghusband on social workers, Mrs Cockburn on housing, Mrs McDougall on mental health, Mr Carrier on demographic problems, and Mr Bird on some intricacies of our tax system.

Conscious as I was of my lack of first-hand knowledge of the major social services, I decided to seek interviews with some of those actually engaged in the work and I chose for this purpose three very different areas—London (the LCC), Leicester, and the County of Cambridgeshire. I was fortunate in obtaining introductions in the first case from Mrs Peggy Jay, in the second from Professor Neustadt, and in the third from Lady Adrian and

7

Mr Michael Pease. All those I approached were generous in giving me their time and took great trouble in telling me the things I wanted to know, for all of which I here express my gratitude. They are in *London*, in addition to Mrs Jay herself (Vice-Chairman of the Welfare Committee and member of the Children's Committee), Mrs Durbin (member of the Housing Committee, a Rent Tribunal, and other bodies), Mr Lloyd Jacob (Head of the General Division of the Welfare Department), Miss Taylor (Chief Inspector of Child Care), and Mr Balchin (Assistant Director of Housing); in *Leicester* Dr Moss (Medical Officer of Health), Mr Powell (Director of Welfare Services), Mr Evans (Children's Officer), and Mr Hadfield (City Housing Manager); in *Cambridge* Dr Tyser (Medical Officer of Health), Miss Valentine (Children's Officer), and Mr Hitch (County Welfare Officer).

Last, but by no means least, I am indebted to Professor W. A. Robson who first proposed that I should write this book and without whose initiative and encouragement it would never have been written.

PART ONE
The first fifty years

*

1

The legacy of the Victorian era

In the first volume of his autobiography Leonard Woolf writes: 'our youth, the years of my generation at Cambridge, coincided with the end and the beginning of a century which was also the end of one era and the beginning of another . . . We found ourselves living in the springtime of a conscious revolt against the social, political, religious, moral, intellectual and artistic institutions, beliefs and standards of our fathers and grandfathers . . . The battle, which was against what for short one may call Victorianism, had not yet been won, and what was so exciting was our feeling that we ourselves were part of the revolution.'[1] This a personal recollection of the authenticity of which there can be no doubt, and it is supported by many historians who have maintained that the death of Queen Victoria marked the close not only of a reign but of an epoch.[2] But when we pause to consider these sweeping generalizations we remember how often young men of one generation have believed that they were waging a revolutionary war against the generation of their elders, and how many 'epochs' with profoundly significant opening and closing dates historians have discovered, and subsequently discarded. So it behoves us to be cautious; and it is the purpose of this chapter and the next to look at the situation in or around the year 1900 in order to see in what respects if any it really did mark the birth of a new era, especially in the field of social policy.

That year falls midway between what Trevelyan has called 'the two mid-Victorian decades of quiet politics and roaring prosperity'[3] and the appearance of what we have become accustomed to call the Welfare State. For Leonard Woolf it was the time of *Sowing* (the title of his book). Can we transfer the metaphor from his personal life to our social and political history? This would imply that the seed was sown, around the turn of the century, in land that had been ploughed by an earlier generation, and that the harvest was gathered by a later one. We shall see, as we follow the passage of events from the first period to the last, that the metaphor is, in many ways, a very appropriate one indeed.

The industrial revolution, whatever may be the truth about its beginning, most certainly had no end. For it is the essence of industrialization that, once you are well 'over the hump', and fully committed to the industrial way of life, the movement never stops and (in all probability) the pace will get continually hotter. It takes a society a little time to get accustomed to the motion and to tidy up the bits and pieces which were thrown out of place when the acceleration started. The thesis, just quoted, about the mid-Victorian decades signifies that by then Britain had achieved this adaptation and found its balance, or at least that most of the people who mattered believed that this was so. In a sense they were right, but in another sense they were wrong. It was true that by the 1850's the old order had vanished and a new order had taken its place. It was true, also, that the more violent disturbances which had accompanied its birth were over and that relative harmony prevailed. But much still remained to be done to enable the immanent principles of the new order to reach fulfilment. And when Victorian society, in its age of confidence, embarked upon this task of fulfilment, it set in motion forces within the system itself which led, by natural and logical processes, to its transformation into something totally unforeseen and unfamiliar. In fact, the transformation, when it came, was shaped by a conscious effort on the part of the twentieth-century policy to create a social order essentially different from that of the Victorians.

So far as industry was concerned, the triumph of the Victorian society was beyond dispute. 'The country regarded itself', says Ensor, 'as "the workshop of the world"—a phrase then universal which expressed not an aspiration but a fact.'[4] The boast was justified, but there were, nevertheless, two vital matters to be settled within the industrial system itself, namely the structure of the large business unit and the status of the organizations of the workers that these business units employed. A decisive step towards the settlement of the former was taken when Parliament, in 1855–6, established the legal basis for the operation of joint-stock companies with limited liability. There were some exclamations of horror from *The Times*, but the new shape of things was soon generally accepted. Some years later legislation, culminating in the Act of 1875, legalized collective bargaining by trade unions including (so it seemed) the right to strike. This, too, appeared to be in tune with the spirit of the age. For did not the Royal Commission on Labour, of 1894, express the view that the 'occasional great trade conflict' to settle a major issue represented 'a higher stage of civilization' than continued local bickerings?[5] But when the trade unions began to make powerful use of their new liberties, these were challenged by the courts, and had to be reaffirmed, and strengthened, by Parliament in 1906. The truth, not fully realized at the time, was that an industrial system characterized by the consolidation of business into vast impersonal units and the combination of workers into national trade unions was a very different thing from the paradise of individual enterprise, free competition, and self-help which the Victorians imagined they had established. The logical elaboration of the principles of the Victorians, and the natural growth of the institutions they had founded, were leading to something which, though it might at first look like a fulfilment, was in fact a transformation. The seed sown in the ground which the Victorians had ploughed produced a crop unlike anything they had known or could easily imagine.

If capitalist industry was one of the pillars upholding the Victorian system, the other was responsible government, both central and local. After 1832 the cabinet was responsible to a House of Commons, which in turn was aware of its responsibilities to the electorate, but it did not represent the people. The franchise was far too restricted for that. Only about 19% of the adult males in the population had the vote, but the principle that men were sent to Parliament by the votes of their fellow-citizens had been accepted, and it was logically inevitable that, by a process of natural growth, parliamentary government should become representative as well as responsible. The mid-Victorians themselves took the crucial step in 1867 when they passed the Reform Act which just about doubled the proportion of the enfranchised. By the end of the century the system fell little short of manhood suffrage, but it was still based ostensibly on the idea that a man was qualified for the franchise by virtue of his substance as reflected in the annual value of his home. It was not until after World War I that the right to vote was recognized as being a right of citizenship as such, to be enjoyed by men and women alike. However, in 1900 there was a legislative organ in sensitive touch with the public conscience and with the new streams of political thought flowing through the minds and from the pens of the Radicals and Socialists. And in the year 1906 the Labour Party first entered the political arena as a fully qualified competitor in the party game. Even contemporaries, without the help that historical perspective gives, saw, and said, that a new era of party politics had begun. Here, too, natural growth and logical processes were on the way to produce a transformation.

In local government, a matter of great importance in the history of social policy, the picture is not so clear nor the story so simple. The reformed Parliament had cleaned up what *The Times* once referred to as the 'chartered hogsties' of municipal government as early as 1835,[6] but no comparable reform had been undertaken in rural areas when the mid-Victorian age of prosperity and confidence began. Nor did the mid-Victorians make good this defect. When a new task emerged which required a firm hand and an honest mind to guide it they created new machinery for the purpose, first the Poor Law Guardians (with their special administrative areas) and then in 1870 the School Boards, while the urban Sanitary Authorities, under the permissive Act of 1848, largely created themselves by Private Bill very much as the fancy moved them. It is tempting to imagine that the 'sowing' could not have taken place had the ground not been prepared by the legislation which, between the years 1882 and 1894, brought the municipal corporations up to date and established a uniform and effective system of rural administration in the hands of the County, Urban District, and Rural District Councils. But this interpretation cannot really be sustained. For, although a fair measure of concentration of functions in the hands of these bodies did eventually take place, the old tangle remained in being at least till 1929, by which time a new tangle was growing up to take its place, and heated debates about the reform of local government continued to the present day. In fact, in the years around 1900 the only local government that could be counted as a power in the land was municipal government in the cities, together with the specialized bodies just mentioned.

Turning now to the social policy which was enacted and executed by these political organs, it is convenient—since space does not allow a comprehensive survey—to group the salient features of the picture under four headings: education, industry, poverty, and health. Education falls outside the scope of this book because it is the subject of another volume in the series, but a word must be said about it here, if only because it illustrates so well the thesis that natural growth in the second half of the nineteenth century prepared the way for transformation in the twentieth. For the Victorians, democracy and education were partners. A free society could not be orderly unless it was literate, and a self-governing society could not progress in peace unless it was educated. Since, therefore, education was required as much for the benefit of the society as for that of the individual, it was not too difficult to establish the case for holding the State responsible for seeing that it was both offered and accepted. Universal, compulsory, and, therefore, free elementary education was the corollary; it was implicit in the Act of 1870 and was made explicit in subsequent legislation. Thereupon some people concluded that, with democracy and education securely established, there was little more to be done in the way of social policy. But they were wrong even as regards education itself. Attention was next turned, naturally and logically, to technical and secondary education. And then the story of trade unionism repeated itself. The authorities which tried tentatively to invade the field of secondary education were told by the courts that they had no legal power to use public money in this way. In the counter-attack of the Act of 1902 they not only won back the ground they had lost but established a base for further advances in great depth. The eventual result was, once more, a transformation. The public elementary education of the nineteenth century was an inferior commodity provided for an inferior class. The twentieth century introduced the new and penetrating principle of equal opportunity, the effects of which are still working themselves out today in an educational system profoundly different from that of a century ago.

When we look at industry, we see that the mid-Victorian State had already accepted its duty and asserted its right to intervene directly for the protection of workers in factories. It is true that, in accordance with the pure doctrine of individualism as understood at the time, it did not 'interfere' with the liberty of adult male workers but confined its attention (in theory) to women and children. In effect, as was quite clearly appreciated, the men benefited indirectly from some of the measures designed for the protection of the others. As the need to guard the workers not only against moving machinery but also against such insidious menaces to health as lead poisoning and noxious dust became more and more apparent, this principle was quietly dropped in the legislation of the nineties dealing with matters of this kind. The significance of this departure from doctrinaire individualism is considerable, but it should not be misinterpreted. It did not mean that in future individualism was to be replaced by paternalism everywhere. Far from it. It meant only that paternalism was deemed acceptable in cases where the individual was powerless to protect himself, even if he wanted to, and where the ill-judged acts of the few might cause grave injury to the many. Each case must be judged on its merits, and many important instances could be cited, from that time to the present, in which the choice between individualism and paternalism proved difficult and the judgement was not unanimous. We shall meet such instances shortly in the field of Public Health.

But two other aspects of factory legislation are still more important. The first is the creation of the inspectorate, acting under the orders of the central government. We shall return later to the role of inspectors in nineteenth-century social administration. The point about the factory inspectors is that there was no local authority for them to work through; all power was concentrated at the centre, and this was done because it was clearly realized that 'conflicting interests, local influences, indisposition to carrying the law into effect, and other circumstances' might well make administration by local authorities ineffective, as indeed it proved to be when it was tried briefly in the case of workshops as distinct from factories.[7] Secondly, under this legislation first the factories, then the workshops, and eventually even the domestic premises of the manufacturers—that is to say their private property, their real estate, and, in certain circumstances, their homes—were treated as things for the use of which they could be publicly answerable and into which public officials had the right of entry in the ordinary course of their duty. In this way the second great principle of Victorian individualism, the principle of the inviolability of private property, was put on trial and found wanting. Certainly it was not overthrown, but it was dislodged from its position as a sacred dogma and made to submit, like other humbler principles, to the modifications required by the circumstances in which it was applied.

Poverty is a subject that will figure so extensively in the later parts

of this book that little need be said about it here. We can confine
ourselves to identifying the concepts of poverty and of the Poor
Law which prevailed during the period of Victorian confidence,
within the framework of the concept of competitive capitalism.
Poverty, one might venture to say, was regarded more as a social
fact than a social problem. The problem was how to reduce the
mass of apparent or self-declared poverty to the hard core of the
genuine article. This was done by means of the deterrent effect of
the workhouse test and the principles of 'less eligibility' (the condition of the pauper must be less attractive than that of the poorest
person outside this category). This remained the accepted doctrine
in official circles right through the period of confidence and for
some time afterwards. But on the question what to do with the
hard core of genuine poverty there were some doubts and some disagreement. Should they be treated harshly or generously, in the
workhouse or outside it, as unfortunate citizens or as social out-
casts? The answers were not clear, and in the soil of this perturba-
tion of mind lay the seeds of the first great social reforms of the
twentieth century.

There are two points of general significance which must be grasped
if the events that followed are to be understood. The Victorians, we
have just suggested, regarded poverty as a social fact. The poor,
they reflected, are always with us, always have been and always will
be. In the prosperous nineteenth century there should be less,
rather than more, of them than at previous times. Their ever-
present need was traditionally relieved by their families, the Church,
the religious orders, and the neighbours. It was only in a supplementary way, to co-ordinate or to provide special types of service,
that the public authorities stepped in. This is what one sees very
clearly when one looks at a country like France in which religious
institutions operated at full strength, or at the United States, particularly in the early years of its independence, where the neighbourhood generally felt quite capable of looking after its own affairs.
But in Britain the power of religious institutions had been greatly
curtailed by the Reformation, and the strength of the neighbourhood had been extensively undermined by the industrial revolution.
In addition, for centuries the neighbourhood had been personified,
for major administrative purposes, in the Justice of the Peace, who,
though a genuine neighbour, was at the same time a public official
and the agent of the central government. Now the Justices had been
replaced by the Poor Law Guardians who, although still local

worthies, seemed to have even less of the neighbourly spirit in them. Thus the traditional philosophy of poverty still persisted, but the social and institutional structure through which the philosophy could be translated into action had passed away.

The second point to grasp is that we must think in terms not of the poor but of the paupers. Pauperism was a status, entry into which affected not merely a part of a man's life, but the whole of it. He became a pauper for all purposes, and he carried his family with him. Paupers formed a distinct group of second-class citizens, deprived of the most important rights of citizenship. The principal officer of the Poor Law Division of the Local Government Board, giving evidence before the Royal Commission of 1905–9, said that the status of pauper implied 'firstly, the loss of personal reputation (what is understood as the stigma of pauperism); secondly, the loss of personal freedom, which is secured by detention in a workhouse; and thirdly the loss of political freedom by suffering disfranchisement'. The pauper, he added, has in practice a right of relief, but 'his right is not a complete right for the necessary sanctions are lacking . . . he cannot sue for his relief', and that is precisely why it was the duty of the State to see that he gets his rights.[8] The comprehensive character of the status meant that certain essential services, especially those of health and education, were split in two. Sick and infirm paupers were attended by the Poor Law Medical Officer or entered the Poor Law Infirmary, and their children were sent to the Poor Law Schools or other establishments certified as available to them, while the other needy members of the society were provided for by the local Sanitary Authority and its Medical Officer of Health and the local School Board. The anomalies that resulted, as well as the hardships induced by the workhouse test and the rigid conception of pauperism, caused growing uneasiness as the nineteenth century drew towards its close, and provoked a frontal attack on the system in the early years of the twentieth.

Our fourth category of social policy, health, will also figure extensively in this book, but in some respects it is the most critical of all to the understanding of the period under review, and must therefore receive careful attention here. It is critical for two reasons: first, because it was most conspicuously in the field of public health that the battle was fought over the relative roles of central and local government and, one might almost say, even over the role of government as such, in the pursuit of welfare. Secondly, whereas the developments in the machinery of democratic government, in

education, in the structure of industry and the processes of collective
bargaining, and in factory legislation, can properly be regarded as
the natural growth and logical evolution of the mid-Victorian
system, it is a debatable question whether the measures taken in
the field of public health were a natural fulfilment of Victorian
democratic capitalism or an attack launched against it. Aneurin
Bevan took the latter view, but he qualified it by adding that the
system was quick to claim the credit for what had been imposed
upon it by its attackers. Public-health measures, he said, have
become part of the system, 'but they do not flow from it. They have
come in spite of it . . . In claiming them, capitalism proudly dis-
plays medals won in the battles it has lost.'[9] The question having been
posed, one must make haste to admit that it cannot be answered.
There are no valid arguments by which one interpretation can be
proved right and the other wrong. And yet even a cursory glance
at British history leaves the impression that the public-health
measures were much less of a natural growth from within the
system than any of the items listed above. They sprang from the
determined efforts of a small number of men—doctors and civil
servants—of outstanding ability, courage, and energy who can easily
be identified as the pioneers of this great advance. They had to
instil into the circles that controlled affairs both in industry and in
local government something of their own knowledge and understanding and of their own attitude to life; their understanding not
only of the medical but also of the social factors involved, and their
attitude towards man's environment, which refused to treat it as
something given, as something to be accepted as an expression of the
unalterable laws of nature. It was equally necessary in this concept-
ualization of the environment, both physical and social, to see in
it something different from a mere aggregation of individual actions
and circumstances to which the principles of individual rights and
freedoms could be applied. The physical environment created by
men and the social environment composed of men must be handled
according to principles peculiar to themselves, and it was for the
recognition and general application of these principles that men
like Chadwick and Southwood Smith were fighting. One of the
most notable examples of the utter failure to grasp this point is
the leading article in *The Times* of 1 August 1854, celebrating
the downfall of these two men and the suppression of the Board of
Health. 'If there is such a thing as a political certainty among us, it
is that nothing autocratic can exist in this country. The British

nature abhors absolute power . . . The Board of Health has fallen.'
And it continues: 'We all of us claim the privilege of changing our
doctors, throwing away their medicine when we are sick of it, or
doing without them altogether whenever we feel tolerably well . . .
Esculapius and Chiron, in the form of Mr Chadwick and Dr
Southwood Smith, have been deposed, and we prefer to take our
chance of cholera and the rest than be bullied into health.'

This passage covers three distinct points. The first is concerned
with the limits of bureaucratic power and in particular with the
relations between the central bureaucracy and the allegedly democratic local authority; we shall return to this in a moment. The second
refers to the right of the individual to choose for himself. But this
is a right which, as we saw in the case of the Factory Acts, applies
only where there is a real power to choose and when the choice
made by one man cannot endanger the health and welfare of others.
The third point concerns the environment and is a complete *non
sequitur*. It would have been impossible to cope with 'cholera and
the rest' without the help of bureaucracy guided by the best scientific
knowledge of the age, and the man who decided to 'take his chance'
was a menace to the health of his neighbours. Fortunately *The
Times*' song of victory was premature, and the public-health movement continued to advance. Legislation had begun in 1848, after
preliminary investigations into the state of the towns, and the first
phase of advance ended with the 'Great Public Health Act' of 1875.
This defined the responsibilities and powers of the local Sanitary
Authorities and the functions of the Medical Officer of Health, an
official whose appointment in every area was at least 'nominally
compulsory'.[10] In the closely related field of housing legislation the
Act of 1868 decreed that the owner of a house condemned by the
MOH could be compelled to reconstruct it or pay for its reconstruction. Then in 1875 explicit recognition was given to the environmental principle in the 'Cross Act' which empowered the local
authority to clear a slum area, and in the process to demolish houses
which were not themselves unfit for habitation but whose removal
was necessary for the replanning of the area. In the next phase the
focus shifted to the individual and his treatment, and new contro-
versies arose, for, as Professor Mackintosh has said, 'the difficulty
experienced by people of goodwill towards the condition of the new
poor was that the movement from environmental to personal health
measures involved a principle which they were loth to concede'.[11]

Before we close this chapter there is one question to be considered which is relevant to all areas of social policy. It is the question of the means by which a central government (1) gathers information about the social problems with which the policy is to deal; (2) having decided on its policy, explains to its local executives, whether they are its own servants or autonomous local authorities, what they are to do; (3) keeps a watch to see if they are doing it, and (4) puts pressure on them, if they are not, to make them do it. Some provision to meet these needs is a prerequisite of any social policy, and it is therefore important to know whether the twentieth century inherited from the nineteenth a serviceable equipment for these purposes. The answer to (1) is the almost fabulous list of reports of Royal Commissions and Select Committees, admittedly somewhat unequal in quality, which were one of the outstanding contributions of the period to the apparatus of government. The answer to questions (2) and (3) is, apart from routine Ministry circulars, the inspectorate. There were inspectors for the Factory Acts, for education, for the Poor Law (Assistant Commissioners), and for Public Health. Their relations with the local executives of policy varied. The factory inspectors had no local agents to work through. For education and the Poor Law there were the *ad hoc* Boards created by government for the purpose, and therefore having something of the character of government agents. In Public Health the Sanitary Authorities were an integral part of general local government, and often showed the independence character-istic of its institutions. But, whoever it was that they were dealing with, the inspectors occupied a key position which they exploited to the full. In his book on mid-Victorian administration David Roberts gives us the fullest portrait of them and their work that we have yet had.[12] They included in their ranks man of outstanding character and ability, having among them at one time eleven who became Fellows of the Royal Society. They saw everything and could swing their influence in both directions, now on the centre and now on the regions, and in doing so they often did not act merely as go-betweens but drew heavily on their own experience and opin-ions. But their power was limited, and its limitation was rooted in the fundamental ideas of the time about the liberties of the subject in a free society and the relations between central and local govern-ment. The accepted pattern of action consisted of inspection, report, and advice. The inspectors of mines were told to 'afford to any parties who may solicit it . . . advice and suggestions', but to abstain from dictation; for 'persuasion not coercion was the ideal of the Victorian administrators'.[13] So the answer to point (4) (how did the central government put pressure on the local agents to execute its policy?) is that the pressure was exerted rather patchily, often indirectly, and not always effectively. But the result was better than might have been expected. The inspectors were skilful and persuasive, public opinion was being gradually enlisted on the side of social progress, and in the last resort compulsion could be used. But few departments of government could issue and enforce their own rules and regulations, so compulsion had to take the form of a prosecution in the Civil Courts, which was a cumbersome and uncertain procedure. The courts were likely to observe the letter rather than the spirit of the law, as they did for several years when confronted by systematic evasion (by the use of labour shifts) of the known intention of the Ten Hours Act of 1847. It was some time before the strong dislike of bureaucratic authority backed by coercive power could be suffciently overcome to permit the fully effective execution of social policy.

In the mid-Victorian age of confidence there was a continuous resistance to the encroachment of the central government in local affairs, but the encroachment went on. The machinery at the centre was steadily expanding, and we are told that the twenty years ending in 1854 saw the addition of twenty permanent central agencies to the apparatus. Also, even when no uniform pattern could be imposed by authority on the local administration, the device was used with considerable effect of designing models which most of the local authorities were only too glad to copy. So, by the time the period of confidence ended and the nineteenth century drew to a close, the ideas, the habits, and the machinery of government had developed to a point at which the obstacles to the new urge in social policy were not insuperable. Whatever we may think about the exact interpretation of the phrase 'The Welfare State', we can appreciate the force in David Roberts' judgement that during the mid-Victorian epoch the ordinary Englishman had become 'the beneficiary of a state that assumed a responsibility for the well-being of its citizens. However limited that responsibility, however meagre compared to the responsibilities assumed by Whitehall today, it did mark the beginning of the Welfare State.'[14]

1 Leonard Woolf, *Sowing*, pp. 151 and 160
2 e.g. J. A. R. Marriott, *Modern England 1885–1932*, p. 155
3 G. M. Trevelyan, *History of England*, p. 50
4 R. C. K. Ensor, *England 1870–1914*, p. 109
5 Royal Commission on Labour, 1894, vol. XXXV, p. 36
6 Cited by Sir Ivor Jennings in H. J. Laski (ed.), *A Century of Municipal Progress*, p. 57
7 Children's Employment Commissioners, 1864, quoted in B. L. Hutchins and A. Harrison, *A History of Factory Legislation*, p. 224
8 Harold E. Raynes, *Social Security in Britain*, p. 175
9 A. Bevan, *In Place of Fear*, pp. 73–4
10 W. M. Frazer, *A History of English Public Health 1834–1939*, p. 121
11 J. M. Mackintosh, *Trends of Opinion about the Public Health, 1901–1951*, p. 30
12 David Roberts, *Victorian Origins of the British Welfare State*
13 ibid., p. 287
14 ibid., p. 315

2

Problems and policies at the turn of the century

It was argued in the last chapter that during the period of Victorian confidence in the social order the ground was being prepared for the new developments of the twentieth century in part by the natural and logical evolution of the social order itself. But in the last quarter of the nineteenth century the situation was changed by a series of events and discoveries which severely shook the confidence of the Victorians and seemed to betray unsuspected weaknesses in their society. One of the most important effects was to provide fresh ammunition and a more receptive audience for the various critics of the system whose utterances until then had not greatly disturbed the general calm, but who were now in a position to challenge the dominant orthodoxy. The distinction here made between events and discoveries may be a little arbitrary, but it is useful. It serves to distinguish between occurrences which struck society with a new impact, and the fruits of deliberate, planned enquiries which revealed conditions that had existed for some time, and thus convicted the public mind of having been lulled into a false complacency.

The principal event was the depression which attacked the economy of the Western world in the last quarter of the century. In Britain it came at a time when the competition of foreign industries had made manufacturers doubt whether the country was still entitled to call itself the 'workshop of the world', and it was accompanied by the new and alarming phenomenon of mass unemployment. In 1882, in spite of the gathering clouds, the *Spectator* could write: 'Britain as a whole never was more tranquil and happy. No class is at war with society or the government: there is no disaffection anywhere, the Treasury is fairly full, the accumulations of capital are vast.'[1] Very soon, however, the unemployed were demonstrating in Hyde Park, and in 1886 Hyndman, leader of the Marxist wing of the Socialist forces, was addressing packed crowds in

Trafalgar Square, with John Burns waving a red flag and shouting, 'When we give the word for a rising will you join us?' There followed rioting, arrests, prosecutions, and—most significantly—acquittals. The Mansion House fund for the unemployed, 'which had long lingered, half moribund, at about £3,000, rose in the four days after the riot to £20,000', and a fortnight later reached £60,000.[2] This was tangible evidence of the extent of public sympathy. The corresponding crisis in the United States came a little later, in the years 1894 to 1898, when the percentage of unemployed in manufacturing industry and transport rose from a level of around 5% to a maximum of 16·7%, and the depression was described as 'extreme', 'deep', severe', and 'intense'.[3] The comments of historians on events in the two countries are very similar. In England, says Ensor, 'the slump gave Victorian courage and optimism the severest shock that it had yet received'.[4] In the United States, we are told, 'it was clear that the country was being profoundly shaken, that men everywhere were beginning to envisage a turning-point in national development'.[5]

The shaking engendered a new attitude to social problems. According to the old orthodoxy the prime cause of social distress and destitution was to be found in the persons or individual circumstances of the victims, and it was usually identifiable as moral weakness. There was considerable resistance to admitting the presence of impersonal social causes, because this implied an inherent defect in the system itself. The shock administered by the spectacle of mass unemployment did much to break this resistance, because it was evident that the unemployed in Trafalgar Square were not a collection of weaklings or idlers, but the product of an impersonal phenomenon called 'unemployment', a word that had only recently been introduced into the vocabulary. Close on the heels of these events came the famous strikes of the match-girls and the dockers, in 1888–92, in which once more public sympathy was on the side of those protesting against their lot. And this time it was not a question of people who had been ejected from an economic system which, for the moment at least, had no use for them. The complaints were voiced by men and women whose labour was in demand but who were not thereby enabled to rescue themselves from conditions of extreme poverty.

In this sense these strikes were not only events; they were also discoveries. They brought to light new facts about the standard of living of the unskilled workers. And they coincided in time with other discoveries of still wider import. These did not leak out; they burst out with sudden and dramatic force from several directions at once. The most celebrated, though not the first,* sources of the new enlightenment were Charles Booth's study of the people of London, the first volume of which appeared in 1889, and Seebohm Rowntree's similar study of York, published in 1902. These books created a sensation, and the facts reported in them passed immediately into general currency as established truths, and were quoted with telling effect in the highest circles. 'We know, thanks to the patience and accurate scientific investigations of Mr Rowntree and Mr Charles Booth, that there is about 30% of our population underfed, on the verge of hunger.' So wrote Leo Chiozza Money in his widely read and very influential book *Riches and Poverty*.[6] The tone is typical; it is that of a man announcing a discovery, not quoting an opinion. And yet these two local studies provided only a slender basis for a general statement of this kind. A little later Lloyd George, at the outset of his campaign for social reform, was equally emphatic. Booth and Rowntree, he said, have 'revealed a state of things, especially in the towns, which it would be difficult even for the orators of discontent to exaggerate. There are ten millions in this country enduring year after year the torture of living while lacking a sufficiency of the bare necessaries of life.'[7] This was in 1906, when the road to old-age pensions and National Insurance still lay ahead of him, beset with hazards both known and unknown; he needed the popular support that these shocking truths might win for his social programme.

A second source of new information to which historians frequently refer is the Report of the Interdepartmental Committee on Physical Deterioration of 1904. It is indeed relevant to the story, but not so much because it administered a shock as because it was set up to investigate a shocking discovery which had already been announced. This was the report of the military authorities on the high rate of rejection, on medical and physical grounds, of recruits during the South African war. They concluded from this experience that the physical state of the population had deteriorated. The Interdepartmental Committee, on the contrary, decided that it had not. The statistics, they said, had been mishandled and misinterpreted, and they expressed the hope that their work might have some effect in 'allaying the apprehensions of those who, as it appears on in-

* A famous and influential predecessor was *The Bitter Cry of Outcast London*, 1883

sufficient grounds, have made up their minds that progressive deterioration is to be found among the people generally'.[8] But, on the basis of quite different evidence, they showed that some very shocking conditions existed in certain sections of the population, especially in the poorer parts of the big cities. They made a strong appeal for action to alleviate overcrowding, pollution of the atmosphere and underfeeding, and for the medical inspection of school children.[9]

A third disclosure concerned the sweated industries. It was not so much the report of the House of Lords Committee of 1888 on sweating, though the mere fact of its appointment was full of significance, nor the brilliant study made by Beatrice Webb, that administered a sudden shock to the public mind, but rather the Sweated Industries Exhibition organized by the *Daily News* in 1906. Here could be seen particulars about the hours of work and the earnings of the sweated workers (mostly women and children), examples of the work they produced, demonstrations of the skill and labour they put into it, and models of the rooms in which they toiled. The effect was irresistible. Finally one might add the growing body of knowledge about the housing of the people, although here the story lacks the element of sudden discovery. However, for those who knew the facts, the situation was sufficiently alarming. As far back as 1885 a Royal Commission had reported that, although the improvement in the housing of the poor in the past thirty years had been enormous, 'yet the evils of overcrowding, especially in London, were still a public scandal, and were becoming in certain localities more serious than they ever were'.[10] And in 1900 the Prime Minister was telling the Conservative Party that they should devote all the power they possess to getting rid of that which is really a scandal to our civilization . . . I would earnestly press upon all over whom my opinion may have any weight that the subject which should occupy their attention more than any other social subject is that of providing adequate and healthy accommodation for the working classes.'[11]

Thus the pride of Britain was assaulted from all directions. Her cities were breeding young men unfit to fight for her, there were workers in her industries reduced to conditions to which only a Dickens could do justice, a third of her inhabitants were living in absolute poverty or on the edge of it, and the slums of her towns were a public disgrace. The combined effect of these discoveries was great enough to change the political atmosphere and to create possibilities for new and more determined action. The previous generation had realized that these problems existed, but had not grasped their magnitude. Consequently their treatment of them remained, as it were, peripheral, as though concerned only with the fringes of society and not with large sections of its ordinary members. The new situation demanded a reappraisal of the rights of the citizen and of the obligations of the State towards him.

The recognition of the need for such a reappraisal and the attempts made to meet this need deeply disturbed the political thinking of the period and left their mark on the programmes of the political parties. It is remarkable how often in the speeches and writings of these years one meets the words 'Socialist' and 'Socialism'. It is obvious that the representatives of the old orthodoxy felt it necessary to take up some position with regard to this new doctrine—to belittle it, to appropriate it, or to fight it. And it is equally obvious that many of them had only the vaguest idea what it was; which was not surprising, since even those who called themselves Socialists were not in agreement on this point. Definitions of Socialism varied greatly. Dicey, in his book *Law and Public Opinion in England*, published in 1905, called the years from 1865 to 1900 'The Period of Collectivism', and he defined collectivism as 'the school of opinion often termed (and generally by more or less hostile critics) Socialism, which favours the intervention of the State, even at some sacrifice of individual freedom, for the purpose of conferring benefit upon the mass of the people'.[12] He elaborated the definition by specifying the types of State action he had in mind, and giving examples.

This definition is broad enough to cover practically all the policies of social reform that were taking shape at the turn of the century. For they all sprang from the belief that the State was responsible (in some measure) for the welfare of 'the mass of the people' and that it was endowed with the authority to interfere (to some extent) with individual freedom and economic liberty in order to promote it. The novelty of this idea lay in its divergence from the former view that the State was concerned only with the destitute and the helpless, and that its action on their behalf must not impinge upon the ordinary life of the community. And Dicey was quite right in saying that this was what most people meant by 'socialism'—except, of course, for the real Socialists, who meant much more by it. But he was wrong in suggesting that the term was used mostly by the hostile critics of Socialism. It is true that 'Tory Socialist' was originally a term of abuse applied to those Conservatives whose humanitarian feelings had enticed them along paths which seemed to lead straight to Radicalism.[13] But the Radicals themselves frankly admitted, or one might almost say proudly claimed, that their programme was compounded of Socialism. To Dicey the 1885 programme was merely moving 'in the direction of socialism',[14] but Joseph Chamberlain, its principal author, was more emphatic. The aim of the Radicals was, he said, a government 'in which all shall co-operate in order to secure to every man his natural rights, his right to existence, and to a fair enjoyment of it. I shall be told tomorrow that this is Socialism . . . of course it is Socialism. The Poor Law is Socialism; the Education Act is Socialism; the greater part of the municipal work is Socialism; and every kindly act of legislation, by which the community has sought to discharge its responsibilities and obligations to the poor, is Socialism; but it is none the worse for that.'[15]

The thinking behind this statement is confused, but the sentiment and the intention are clear. It was becoming necessary to assert a belief in the responsibility of government for the welfare of the people and to deny to the official Socialists any monopoly of good intentions by borrowing their name and rendering it innocuous. Hubert Bland, the Fabian, put the point very clearly in his comment on the famous utterance of a leading Liberal. 'Why does that extremely well oiled and accurately poised weathercock, Sir William Harcourt, pointing to the dawn, crow out that "we are all Socialists now"?' And his answer to his own question was that no politician could address a political meeting at that time without making some reference 'of a socialist sort to the social problem'.[16] Naturally this kind of talk angered the Socialists proper, because it obscured the real nature of the conflict of opinion. They were not at war with Tory Socialists or Radical Socialists, and were even prepared to support them when they agreed on particular measures. But they were the implacable enemies of the traditional Liberalism of the nineteenth century, the Liberalism of Gladstone and *laissez-faire*. And they thought, and hoped, that it was dying.

In 1889 the *Nineteenth Century* published a symposium of articles on the 'Liberal Collapse'. 'The Liberal Party', wrote Sidney Low, 'is once more in trouble about its soul,' and Keir Hardie and Ramsay MacDonald, speaking for the Independent Labour Party, explained what the trouble was. Liberalism had assumed that 'the man politically enfranchised would be economically free; but experience was proving that the hope was thoroughly false, and Liberalism had nothing else to put in its place'.[17] And three years later Sidney Webb returned to this theme in the same journal. Gladstonian Liberalism, he said, was extinct because it had an 'atomic conception of society'. 'Its worship of individual liberty evokes no enthusiasm. Its reliance on "freedom of contract" and "supply and demand" . . . now seems to work out disastrously for the masses,' because they lack the means to make their demand effective even for the minimum conditions of well-being. The freedom which the ordinary man now wants 'is not individual but corporate freedom'.[18]

But, though Gladstonian Liberalism might be defunct, a new Liberalism was arising which, under the leadership of Asquith, Lloyd George, and Winston Churchill, was destined to carry social policy forward on the first stage of its journey towards the Welfare State. It accepted fully that common element in the new outlook which Chamberlain and others called 'socialist'. Churchill, in 1906, declared that 'the fortunes and the interests of Liberalism and Labour are inseparably interwoven; they rise from the same forces'. And he urged his followers not to be discouraged if some old woman came along and told them their measures were 'socialistic'. He even admitted that 'the whole tendency of civilization is . . . towards the multiplication of the collective functions of society', but he insisted nevertheless that the Liberalism he championed was in essence the very antithesis of Socialism, because Liberalism wanted only to humanize the system of free enterprise, whereas Socialism would destroy it.[19] For by 1906 the question was no longer whether the State was responsible for the welfare of the masses, instead of merely for the relief of the destitute. This was generally agreed, and after all the masses now had the vote. The problem was to decide on the extent of the responsibility and above all on the means by which it should be discharged. And here consensus ended and political conflict began. And when we look more closely at the clash of opinions we shall see that the issues raised were fundamentally the same then as they are now.

We can identify three main schools of thought. First there is the genuine Socialist school. This starts from the belief that the 'capitalist system' of private enterprise and a free market economy is inefficient and unjust. It is a kind of anarchy that should be replaced by a rational order of things planned and directed by the political power. In such an order, not only would the normal needs of everybody be met automatically by the operation of the system itself, but many of the needs that now clamour for satisfaction would no longer exist, since their cause—primarily poverty, squalor, and insanitary conditions of life—would be eliminated. Social progress, therefore, should be marked by a reduction, not an increase, in the special social services which are extraneous and supplementary to the working of the social and economic system itself.

This was the line of thought pursued at first by the Fabians. They had so much faith in the efficiency of a Socialist economy that they paid little attention to social policy as such. They thought that under Socialism, most of our social problems would disappear. Sidney Webb, looking back in 1920 at those early pioneering days of simple enthusiasm, admitted that he and his friends had behaved 'as if society were, or ought to be, composed entirely of healthy adults, free from accidents and exempt, if not from death, at any rate from senility'.[20] This is, no doubt, a piece of deliberate self parody, but it is true that Graham Wallas, in his chapter in the original *Fabian Essays*, had dismissed very lightly the whole question of those who, in a Socialist society, would be unable to provide for themselves. 'There would always remain the sick, and infirm, and the school children, whose wants would be satisfied from the general stock without asking them to bear any part of the general burden.'[21] The essential thing was to socialize the system itself.

The second school of thought was the most strongly represented at the time. Its adherents admitted that the economic system left many needs unsatisfied and distributed its rewards inequitably, but held that in the purely economic tasks of production and distribution of goods it was superior to anything else that might be put in its place. They therefore did not wish to see any drastic change in the system. But, since they believed that the system could not cure its social defects itself, they recognized the responsibility and the right of the State to interfere and compulsorily to modify and supplement its operations. For the members of this school of thought, therefore, the first task of the twentieth century was to extend the social services and increase what Churchill called the 'collective functions' of society, until the ideal balance between private enterprise and public provision and control was attained. The outstanding examples of this approach to the problem are the Radical programme of 1885 and the Liberal programme of 1906.

The third school of thought was of less importance, because its influence was declining. It was that of the Conservatives who thought that there was nothing seriously wrong with the economic system and that the main concern of government should be to see that it had every facility and encouragement to continue its good work. If everybody worked hard, cared for their children, and saved up for sickness and old age, the volume of cases requiring, and deserving, outside help would be small. Public social services, except for a strictly administered Poor Law, were likely to diminish the incentive to work and save. Therefore it would be best to leave as much as possible of the welfare work to the voluntary agencies. This was the basic philosophy of the Charity Organization Society, the most important voluntary agency of the time. It rested on the belief that England was a rich and prosperous country, and that, where wealth abounded, poverty must be unnecessary. Mrs Bosanquet, a leading exponent of the doctrine, asserted that all who were not genuinely incapable of work should be held responsible for their own maintenance and that of their dependent relatives. It may be asked, she said, 'what if the social conditions will not permit them to meet the responsibility?' And her answer was—'It is a vain and idle hypothesis. The social conditions *will* permit them.'[22]

Some of the views associated with the COS were peculiar to it and were rapidly losing ground among those in a position to influence policy. Canon Barnett, for instance, at one time an active member, was driven by his disapproval of the narrow-minded harshness prevalent in the organization to resign from the committee. 'They were just impossible,' he wrote of the members he had met at the meeting, 'refusing to do anything except clothe themselves in the dirty rags of their own righteousness.'[23] But the crux of the matter for this school of thought as a whole was the contention that the State should not interfere with the economic system nor try compulsorily to modify its working. It should remain outside the arena in which the economic battle went on and confine itself to picking up the casualties. Charles Booth, as a convinced Liberal and anti-Socialist, was naturally inclined to favour this view, but he was not satisfied with the ordinarily accepted way of applying it. He agreed that the infiltration of social services into the population at large would be likely to destroy the springs of individual effort, but he thought the State should assume a greater responsibility for those who really needed its help. So he invented the compromise that he called 'limited socialism'. He proposed that all those incapable of providing for themselves should become wards of the State, living in industrial colonies where their livelihood was guaranteed. This would leave the rest of the society free from any interference with individual enterprise, competition, and self-help. 'Our individualism fails', he wrote, 'because our socialism is incomplete.'[24] The determination to keep measures of social help and welfare right outside the frontiers of the economic system could hardly be carried further than this. But very soon the sheer weight of the evidence forced him to abandon this pipe-dream, and to put forward his famous proposal of non-contributory old-age pensions of five shillings a week for everybody and no questions asked.

These three points of view are deeply rooted in the very nature of modern society and the issues they raise have therefore remained alive to this day, though in a setting that has gradually changed. The dividing line between the first and the second—the 'revolutionary' and the 'reformist'—came to fall, not between the Socialists and the rest, but within the Socialist movement itself. On the one hand were those who continued to maintain that the only policy acceptable to Socialism was one that aimed at the elimination of the capitalist system. Social welfare measures were merely palliatives, which sapped the strength of the attack on capitalism. On the other side were those who became increasingly interested in, and favourable to, social legislation that humanized the capitalist system without overthrowing it. The Fabians moved in that direction, as Sidney Webb's remark quoted above indicates, although they were at first strongly opposed to compulsory insurance. And much later, as we shall see, the Labour Party became the most ardent champions of the Welfare State.

The second point of view, which favoured welfare measures, was of course held also by many non-Socialists; by Radicals in general and by those Liberals who had escaped from the strait-jacket of nineteenth-century dogmatism. They had been given a lead by the distinguished economist Stanley Jevons, who argued in favour of judging practical issues on their merits and not by appealing to the authority of some doctrine. 'In social philosophy,' he wrote, 'or rather in practical legislation, the first step is to throw aside all supposed absolute rights or inflexible principles', even the principles of liberty and property. 'I conceive', he continued, 'that the State is justified in passing any law, or even in doing any single act which, without ulterior consequences, adds to the sum total of happiness.'[25] The view was also held by many Conservatives for humanitarian reasons, and by some, perhaps, for the rather more subtle reason given by Arthur Balfour. 'Social legislation, as I conceive it,' he said, 'is not merely to be distinguished from Socialist legislation, but it is its most direct opposite and its most effective antidote.'[26]

The third point of view carried diminishing weight as the social policy of the twentieth century developed, but it has recently re-appeared in a modified form, as a result of the alleged arrival on the scene of the Affluent Society. It is argued that amid so much affluence poverty can be only an exceptional phenomenon, and that now it really is possible (as Mrs Bosanquet wrongly believed it to be half a century earlier) for all but a few to win for themselves all the amenities of a civilized existence.

1   Edward R. Pease, *The History of the Fabian Society*, p. 13
2   Godfrey Elton, *England Arise!*, pp. 123–30
3   John R. Commons, *History of Labour in the United States*, vol. III, pp. 128 and 219
4   R. C. K. Ensor, *England 1870–1914*, p. 111
5   Richard Hofstadter, *The Age of Reform*, p. 166
6   L. G. Chiozza Money, *Riches and Poverty*, p. 5
7   D. Lloyd George, *Slings and Arrows*, p. 6
8   Parliamentary Papers, 1904, vol. XXXII, p. 92
9   ibid., p. 72
10 Royal Commission on the Housing of the Working Classes, First Report, 1885, p. 4 (Cmd. 4402)
11 J. M. Mackintosh, *Trends of Opinion about the Public Health, 1901–1951*, pp. 42–3
12 A. V. Dicey, *Law and Public Opinion in England during the Nineteenth Century*, 1919, p. 64
13 R. L. Hill, *Toryism and the People*, pp. 5–6
14 Dicey, op. cit., p. 256
15 S. MacCoby, *The English Radical Tradition 1763–1914*, pp. 201–2
16 *Fabian Essays* (Jubilee Edition, 1948), pp. 194–7
17 *The Nineteenth Century*, 1899, pp. 10 and 23–7
18 'Lord Rosebery's Escape from Houndsditch' in *The Nineteenth Century*, 1901, p. 366
19 W. S. Churchill, *Liberalism and the Social Problem*, 1909, pp. 71–8
20 *Fabian Essays*, p. xxii
21 ibid., p. 137
22 Helen Bosanquet, *The Strength of the People*, 1903, p. 208
23 Henrietta Barnett, *Canon Barnett, his Life, Work and Friends*, vol. II, p. 265
24 T. S. and M. B. Simey, *Charles Booth*, pp. 193–4
25 Stanley Jevons, *The State in Relation to Labour*, pp. 9 and 12
26 E. Halévy, *History of the English People in the Nineteenth Century*, vol. V, p. 231

3

The problem of poverty

It is not surprising that most countries of the Western world should have felt, towards the end of the nineteenth century, that their methods of dealing with poverty were in urgent need of revision. The new information which was being accumulated revealed not only the true magnitude of the problem but also the great heterogeneity of the company of paupers. Where the Poor Law had been for centuries the only public agency for giving assistance to the helpless and destitute, as well as 'correcting' the idle and insubordinate, it had become a multi-purpose affair without having developed a variety of methods corresponding to the variety of cases with which it had to deal. The relief of poverty, too, was a field of action in which both public and voluntary bodies were active, often with a fairly equal distribution of responsibility between the two. And the public authorities concerned were mostly local ones. Thus there was a need both to co-ordinate the services and to standardize the procedures of the various agencies, and this was particularly necessary where urbanization was changing the nature of the problems and making some of the old methods of dealing with them obsolete.

In facing this task Britain suffered more acutely than any other country from the unhappy legacy of its nineteenth-century system. Nowhere else could you find quite the same combination of harsh deterrent principles, centralized policy control, and administration by an isolated authority, detached from the normal organs of local government, specializing in the treatment of paupers and nothing but paupers, and functioning in regions peculiar to itself. The Poor Law Guardians lacked both the incentive to modify and humanize their ideas, which the central government obtained from the contemplation of its overall responsibilities, and also the personal touch that one might expect to find in true representatives of a neighbourhood. In fact it was precisely because the parish authorities had been too weak or too fearful to check the spread of indiscriminate relief in the early years of the century that the Poor Law Guardians and their Unions had been invented in 1834. Although in most countries of the Western world there had at one time been a tendency to lump rogues, vagabonds, and paupers together in a single category, and to treat them all in semi-penal institutions, the concept of pauperism as both an inferior and a shameful status persisted longer and penetrated more deeply into the public mind in England than elsewhere. It was kept alive, and deliberately reinforced, by the bureaucratic machinery created to translate it into action.

The situation was different in countries where the dominating influences were those of voluntary and charitable bodies, especially the Churches, or the accepted leaders of local communities. In France, for example, the protagonists in the story were the Church and the Commune. It had been declared by Louis XIV that the estates of the Church were the patrimony of the poor, and ideas about poverty were still coloured by this tradition. The central government recognized that the secular power and initiative in this matter should be located in the Commune. At this level there was an Office of Charity (Bureau de Bienfaisance), usually headed by the Mayor. It was described as the 'representative' of the poor, and it alone was authorized to receive gifts and legacies on their behalf. This notion of 'representation' of the poor was inimical to the concept of poverty as a degradation, but it was entirely in harmony with the principle that all relief was a kind of charity. Another circumstance favouring a higher status for the paupers than in Britain was the acceptance of the rule that relief should be given in the home, whenever possible, which is almost exactly the reverse of the British practice. The idea was that, if the pauper remained at home, his relatives would care for him; if he was put into an institution, they would wash their hands of all responsibility.[1] We find the same principle adopted later in the Scandinavian countries.[2]

Debates about the problem of poverty in twentieth-century Britain revolved around the notion of 'the break-up of the Poor Law', a phrase popularized by the Webbs to denote the recommendations of the Minority Report of the Poor Law Commission of 1909. But, though the phrase may have been invented by the Webbs, they did not originate the process, which had been going on with gathering force throughout the Western world for some years before the Commission came into existence. It did not, however, at that time aim, as the Webbs did, at the total dissolution of the Poor Law and the authorities that administered it. The purpose of the movement was to provide special services for distinct categories, and to do this outside the ambit of the Poor Law. The categories of persons who were being gradually extracted from the heterogeneous company of paupers were the children, the old, the sick, and the unemployed.

The case for the special treatment of children was an obvious one and had long been recognized in most countries by the provision made for their education and for their exclusion from, or protection in, industrial employment. Measures of this kind applied to all children, whether paupers or not, though the education of the paupers might be given, as it often was in Britain, in special pauper schools. At the same time steps were being taken by the Poor Law authorities to get children out of pauper institutions by boarding them out in families or putting them in cottage homes or entrusting them to voluntary organizations. These practices were encouraged in Britain by the strong recommendations made by Mrs Nassau Senior in her report to the Local Government Board in 1873.[3] The combined effect of these two lines of development was to build up the status of children as a special category among paupers, even when they remained technically in the care of the Poor Law. To them must be added the important legislation which initiated the School Medical Service in 1907 and authorized local authorities to provide meals for school children in 1906. These were clearly seen as an encroachment of the education authorities on the preserves of the Poor Law and were therefore the most definite moves in the direction of its 'break-up' so far as children were concerned.

At the turn of the century most countries of the Western world suffered from a guilty conscience about the aged poor. In Britain a whole series of Commissions and Committees were set up to study the problem, and a survey made for the government in 1899, with a supplement in 1908, described the action taken in Russia, Norway, Sweden, Denmark, Germany, Holland, Belgium, France, Italy, Austria, Roumania, and New Zealand.[4] We shall be concerned with the results of this awakening interest in old people in the next chapter. The point to be noted here is that by the end of the nineteenth century it was universally agreed that respectable, 'deserving' old people, who had worked while they could and were now without means, should not be treated as paupers. But the only action that had been taken in Britain by 1900 was to instruct

Guardians not to force such people into the workhouse, and to see that the relief given them in their homes was adequate to their needs.[5]

As regards the sick, it had for some time been noticed in Britain that the services rendered to the paupers by the District Medical Officer, the Poor Law Dispensary, and the Poor Law Infirmary were not very different from those offered to the general public by the Medical Officer of Health and the municipal and voluntary hospitals. The government had recognized the special character of medical relief and treatment by enacting, in 1885, that its receipt through the Poor Law should not carry the stigma of disfranchisement; this implied that the sick poor were not necessarily to be regarded as paupers. It went on, a few years later, to state officially that it had no objection to the Poor Law Infirmaries being used as general hospitals for ordinary citizens, when no other equivalent facilities were available. As in the case of school meals and the school medical service, some of the Guardians saw this as an encroachment on their preserves, and complained that it blurred the distinction between the pauper and the independent citizen. In Manchester, in order to keep this distinction alive, they instructed their officers when speaking of Poor Law institutions for the sick 'to avoid using the word "hospital" or "infirmary", and simply to use the word "workhouse" '.[6]

The fourth distinctive type of poverty was that caused by unemployment. We have already seen how sharply public attention had been drawn to this in the 1880's and how substantial were the emergency relief funds raised by voluntary subscription. The first clear indication of a new official attitude came when Chamberlain, at the Local Government Board, issued a Circular in 1886 to Local Authorities and Boards of Guardians urging the former to utilize voluntary funds to set to work unemployed men referred to them by the latter. The wording of the circular is significant. The men selected by the Guardians were to be those whom 'it is undesirable to send to the workhouse or to treat as subjects for pauper relief', and they were to be given 'work which shall not involve the stigma of pauperism'.[7] Chamberlain's successor, Walter Long, revived this policy and prepared a Bill which became the Unemployed Workmen's Act of 1905. This rendered obligatory in towns of over 50,000 inhabitants what till then had been only permissive. The task was to be undertaken by Distress Committees representing the Councils and the Guardians; but the Act was a failure. The experience showed that temporary work could not confer any permanent benefit.

Such, in brief, were the trends leading towards the break-up of the Poor Law which were visible at the beginning of the new century, and they were common to the Western world as a whole. Even in the United States, where the resistance of the States to Federal interference in domestic matters and the passionate belief in individual liberty combined to check the development of social legislation, the same tendency was noted by those devoted to the cause of social welfare. One of these observed that 'the movement to analyse the relief load and to substitute for a general assistance program appropriate provision for certain groups or categories was making real headway before the war',[8] that is to say the First World War. And we must also bear in mind that, already in the 1880's, Bismarck had initiated in Germany the first programme of compulsory social insurance, covering sickness, invalidity, and old-age pensions, and had thus introduced the world to what was destined to be the principle alternative to the Poor Law as a means of maintaining the personal incomes of those unable to earn.

The Royal Commission on the Poor Laws and Relief of Distress was appointed by the Conservative government in 1905, shortly before it fell, and reported to the Liberal government in 1909. Its creators intended it, we are told, to suggest administrative improvements which might make it easier to keep the 'principles of 1834' in operation, but it issued two reports, the more conservative of which (the Majority Report) recommended a substantial modification of those principles, while the more radical Minority Report called loudly for their total rejection. Both Reports delved deeply into matters of policy concerning every social problem in which poverty was a factor, and made a host of practical proposals about all of them. But the immediate effect of their labours on policy was very small indeed. The Liberal government had planned most of its social programme, and already put part of it (old-age pensions) into effect, before the Reports appeared. In fact it was not till March 1911, we are told, that Lloyd George began to read the Reports. By then he was well on with the preparation of his National Insurance Bill and, since both Reports were opposed to compulsory social insurance against sickness and unemployment, they could not help him very much.[9] Nevertheless the two Reports are historical documents of great importance. They give us a picture of informed opinion on the major social problems of the day, and they present most of the arguments that were being advanced for and against new proposals current at the time. In addition the Minority Report, written by Beatrice Webb with the able off-stage help of her husband, planted an idea in the minds of British politicians which was first translated into action when the Poor Law Guardians were abolished in 1929, and finally triumphed—or appeared to do so— when Parliament passed the National Assistance Act (1948) with its opening sentence—'the existing poor law shall cease to have effect'.

The two Reports of the Commission had much in common, as the Webbs admitted. They listed the points of agreement, which included the transfer of the administration of the Poor Law to the ordinary local authorities, the abolition of the general mixed workhouse, the abandonment of the principle of deterrence, the adoption of preventive and curative measures in addition to palliatives (or mere relief), the extension of the public medical services, and the introduction of old-age pensions and some kind of facilities for insurance against unemployment.[10] As a matter of fact they were somewhat over-generous to the Majority. For, while rejecting deterrence in its old form, with its associations of 'harshness and still more of hopelessness', they favoured a mild kind of 'less eligibility' even for the aged, and they did not want medical treatment to be 'so attractive that it may become a species of honourable self-indulgence'.[11] Their view on unemployment insurance was the same as that of the Minority. They recognized very clearly the need for more insurance than was as yet provided by the trade unions and other voluntary bodies, but they were opposed to a compulsory scheme, mainly because of the very unequal distribution of the risk among the various occupations. So they recommended the encouragement of voluntary insurance by State subsidies.[12] Pensions for the old and incapacitated worried them a lot, as their instinct was to rely on personal savings. But the evidence was too strong. They expressed their final view in the rather odd sentence—'we almost seem driven to the conclusion that a new form of insurance is required, which, for want of a better name, we may call Invalidity Insurance', but they left it to others to work out a plan.[13] They said it should be contributory, unlike the scheme just enacted by Parliament, and one must assume that they meant it to be compulsory. The Minority, on the other hand, wanted a more generous non-contributory scheme for pensions at the age of sixty-five.[14] But by that time the Old Age Pensions Act was already in force.

There were two major points of disagreement between the two groups. The first concerned the respective roles of the State and the voluntary agencies. The Majority wanted the latter to be the front line of the attack on poverty, with the public service following behind and taking care of the cases with which voluntary action could not deal. And public assistance was to be deliberately made less attractive than voluntary assistance. The Minority objected strongly to these proposals on two grounds. First, because they held that full responsibility for policy and its execution must rest on the public authority, which should make such use of voluntary helpers and the voluntary agencies as it thought fit. This reflected the Fabian belief in the virtues of scientific planning at the centre. Secondly, they could not accept the principle of discrimination between the deserving poor, who would be the charge of the voluntary agencies, and the less deserving, who would be passed on to the Guardians or their successors. This savoured too much of the attitude characteristic of what Beatrice Webb called 'my friend the enemy—the Charity Organization Society—one of the most typical of mid-Victorian offsprings'.[15]

The second point of disagreement was more fundamental. While both groups favoured the extension of the special public services for the care of the old, the sick, the children, and the unemployed, the Majority believed that there would always remain a residual class of destitute persons who could only be looked after by a Destitution Authority, which they proposed to re-name the 'Public Assistance Committee'. It would not only distribute relief in cash or kind, but would provide for all the needs of those entrusted to its guardianship. The Minority maintained that if the public services were properly developed there would be no such residue, and it would be possible to get rid of both the separate category of pauper and the Destitution Authority. There would be only a temporary and miscellaneous collection of 'omitted cases' deposited through the meshes of the administrative net, which could be disposed of by an official whom they proposed to call the Registrar of Public Assistance, because he would also keep a record of all those receiving assistance of any kind from public funds.

The issues raised here are so vital to our subject that we must look carefully into them and see what arguments were, or could be, advanced in support of the two opposed points of view. It is best to begin with the Minority, because their motives are easier to identify. They had three main reasons for wishing to dispense with a destitution authority. The first sprang from the determination of the Webbs to apply scientific principles to social administration. It was unscientific to treat the poor as an operational category, since poverty was of many different kinds and resulted from many different causes. Scientific administration would split up this heterogeneous mass for purposes of treatment into its distinct component parts.

Secondly, they maintained that social policy should never be satisfied merely to relieve distress; its primary aim must be to prevent it and, failing that, to cure it. A destitution authority could never prevent distress, and could rarely cure it, because it could only touch those who were already destitute; and even the destitute often tried to evade its clutches as long as possible, for fear of the stigma its assistance carried with it. And their third reason was that a destitution authority that catered for all the needs of those entrusted to its care would duplicate the general public services, in a wasteful and inefficient way, as indeed the Poor Law services for the children and the sick were already doing.

The Minority envisaged a widely ranging system of public services, co-ordinated at the local level by the Registrar of Public Assistance. For 'Public Assistance' for them had nothing to do with the relief of the poor as such, but referred to every kind of benefit offered to any class of person by a public agency financed (apart from what the recipients might pay) from public funds. It included, as they explained, the case of the paying patient in the County Lunatic Asylum, of the poor man's wife receiving milk at a nominal charge, of the County Bursary to Oxford, and of compulsory admission to an industrial school.[16] They were not offering everything for nothing, nor did they shrink from the need to empower those administering the services to discipline the unruly. The unemployed man, for instance, who could not at once be placed by a Labour Exchange, would be assigned to a Training Establishment, and for the 'industrial malingerer', who kept coming back for relief after he had been given several chances of work, there would be 'judicial commitment to a Detention Colony'.[17] This was the alternative the Minority preferred to the mass assignment of the undeserving to an inferior category and an inferior status.

The Majority were, no doubt, influenced by the natural inclination to cling to the familiar. A dozen of them had been personally active either in the public service or the voluntary agencies and might be expected to defend what they believed to be good in them. It must also be remembered that a proposal to transfer Poor Law functions to the general public services was a proposal to put your faith in what did not yet exist, or what was in the process of being created while the Commission was sitting. When they began their debates there were no old-age pensions, no health insurance, no un-employment insurance, few homes for the aged (except for the work-houses), few general hospitals under public control (except for the infirmaries); the treatment of mental defectives was in its infancy and was being studied by another Commission; free meals for poor school children, as offered in London, were a novelty regarded with suspicion (until the Act of 1906); Care Committees under the edu-cation authorities were only just beginning to appear; the powers to deal with cruel or negligent parents were quite inadequate (until improved by the Children Act of 1908). The picture drawn by the Minority, or rather by the Webbs, was in fact a brilliant anticipation of the eventual results of a movement which had only just started and of which they sensed the nature, except for their rejection of the instrument of compulsory social insurance.

It is not surprising that the Majority should believe that the resi-due of cases left untended by the specialized public services would be, at least for a long time to come, a large and important one, and that consequently there must continue to be a general assistance agency to deal with them. When one asks what would be the common characteristics of these cases, one comes to the crux of the matter. And here it is best not to try to establish what actually were the motives that influenced the minds of the Majority, but rather to see what their proposals seem to imply.

One of the common characteristics was, of course, extreme poverty. But there was another, closely associated with it, which we might call helplessness, and the Majority were much concerned about this more personal factor. It must be interpreted as covering not only the old, sick, feeble-minded, feckless, idle, and (if children) neglected, but also the incorrigibles who were apparently incapable of living a decent life but were not criminals. All these needed some-thing more than cash benefits, because poverty was not their only problem, and also something more than a specialized service, be-cause their trouble was aggravated by poverty. They were cases, it might be argued, where it was necessary, either for their own benefit or in the public interest or both, that somebody should take charge of their lives. The Majority made it clear that the authority accepting this responsibility should try, not merely to relieve their distress, but also to overcome their helplessness. They also made it clear that even if helplessness were a common characteristic of these cases, they must also be poor. They did not wish the public assistance authority to extend its range of activities beyond those afflicted by poverty. But they proposed a certain enlargement of the definition of the class eligible for assistance by suggesting that it be described as 'necessitous' instead of 'destitute'.[18]

The Majority were also much concerned that the family, in which several different factors might be at work to produce distress, should be treated as a unit. It was a part of the ancient tradition of the Poor Law in Britain and elsewhere that it should deal with families, and not merely with individuals; hence the basic principle, dating from Elizabethan times, that the resources of the family must be taken into account in deciding whether poor relief should be given and, if so, how much. It is true that this principle had some bad consequences, such as the practice of treating the whole family as paupers if the head became a pauper. But it also had its good side, potentially at least, since welfare work is most effective if based upon the family unit. And this was recognized also by the voluntary agencies to which the Majority wished to assign so important a role. They were moving towards the perfection of the techniques of 'family case work' which are so highly esteemed today. But this, said the critics, was precisely what the Minority's plan for reliance on specialized and technical services would exclude. The Webbs were aware of this criticism, and tried to answer it in a long footnote in one of their books. It might be objected, they said, that in 'directing attention to the fact that it is always an individual who is attacked, not, at first, the family as a whole', they were ignoring the case of families which were 'as whole families, in a state of destitution'. Their reply was that 'each member of such a family requires, for restoration, specialized treatment according to his or her need'.[19] But this really missed the point. It was not only a question of what we should now call 'problem families' but also the much wider one of treating all individual cases with due attention to their family setting. And the fear that the specialized services might fail to do this was not groundless. It is generally agreed that the most glaring defects of the policy of the next few decades was the failure to help parents of large families (by family allowances) and the failure to provide medical care for the families of insured persons.

But all this does not necessarily lead to the conclusion that the old Poor Law Guardians had to be preserved under a new name. What was there about them that the Majority considered to be so ndispensable? Was it, perhaps, precisely the fact that they were not 'service'? A public service is run by public servants who minister to the needs of those who are ultimately, though very indirectly, their masters, and who have the right to demand what the public servants are there to supply. But the person for whom a guardian cares is not his master, but his ward. And a ward is placed, or places himself, in the hands of his guardian, who accepts the responsibility of making decisions on his behalf. Thus the 'wards in poverty', as we might call the paupers, had no clear-cut right to demand any particular benefits or attentions from the Poor Law Guardians. The guarantee that their needs would be met rested, not on their right to insist, but on the Guardian's obligation to provide. The only difference between this and charity was that the obligations of the Guardians were legal and those of the purveyors of charity, moral or religious. It was this relationship of dependence, or of ward to guardian, that the Majority appear to have considered necessary for the proper treatment of the 'necessitous', and it was precisely this feature of Public Assistance that the Minority most intensely disliked and wished to abolish.

What we have touched on here is the whole question of the role and the organizations of welfare service in modern society, and in particular their relationship with services for the relief of poverty. The British Poor Law had the functions, but not the spirit, of a welfare service, and the authors of the Minority Report were quite right in urging that it must be uprooted. But when the 'break-up' for which they had campaigned eventually took place, it was found, as we shall see later, that in the process something had disappeared which it was necessary to re-create in a new form. The consequence was that in Britain, unlike most other countries, welfare and the relief of poverty were placed in separate administrative compartments, and we shall in due course be concerned to explore the advantages and disadvantages of this solution of a very difficult problem. But these events lay in the still distant future. Meanwhile the chipping away at the fringes of the Poor Law continued.

An experienced Poor Law administrator remarked in 1912 that 'the movement known as the Breaking-up of the Poor Law has set in with increasing rapidity within the last few years'. His list of measures that had contributed to this movement included the Old Age Pensions Act, school meals, Care Committees, various developments in Public Health, and the setting up of Reformatories and Industrial Schools by the Home Office. He did not mention the

National Insurance Act of the previous year nor the transfer of the care of mental defectives from the Poor Law to a specialized service.[20] At the same time the humanizing of the administration of the Poor Law itself continued. A good example is the instructions issued to the Guardians to the effect that the amount of relief to be given to a household containing children should be measured by 'the normal standard of income on which a woman may reasonably be expected to bring up her family', and that they should give the relief before the family stocks were so depleted 'as to render it impossible to deal with the case without making good the deficiency'.[21] These instructions clearly rejected the principle of less eligibility and endorse a policy of prevention.

All this was in harmony with what was in one or other or both of the two reports of the Royal Commission, but this does not mean that they inspired it. As we have seen, many of the measures were taken before the Reports were published, while others, like National Insurance, were not in accordance with their recommendations. The truth is that in the years during which the Commission was in session the stream of social change began at last to flow freely, and the Commission was part of the stream, not the origin of it. The other most conspicious part was the Liberal government which came to power and declared its purpose during those same years. Its most active spokesmen presented themselves as the heralds of a new age in which social justice would reign supreme. They insisted that their programme of social reform, though necessarily introduced piece by piece, must be regarded as an integral whole which, when completed, would be seen to have had momentous effects. It was a programme, said Churchill in 1908, when describing the first item in it, that 'marks the assertion of an entirely new principle in regard to poverty; and the principle, once asserted, cannot possibly be confined within existing limits'. The question now was, 'Forward or back?' And he made it quite clear that the answer of the government was 'forward'.[22] He meant that old-age pensions would be followed by National Insurance, and other measures besides. He did not know that he would live to see the forward movement culminate some forty years later in the Welfare State.

1   Emily Greene Balch, *Public Assistance of the Poor in France*, 1893
2   George P. Nelson (ed.), *Freedom and Welfare—Social Patterns in the Northern Countries of Europe*, p. 457
3   Jean S. Heywood, *Children in Care*, pp. 71–2

4   *Provision for Old Age by Government Action in Certain European Countries*, P.P. 1899, vol. XCII; *Memorandum on New Zealand and Germany*, 1908, vol. LXXXVIII

5   K. de Schweinitz, *England's Road to Social Security*, p. 180

6   S. and B. Webb, *English Poor Law Policy*, pp. 214-15

7   W. H. Beveridge, *Unemployment—a Problem of Industry*, 1912, pp. 154-6

8   Grace Abbott, *From Relief to Social Security*, p. 17

9   W. J. Braithwaite, *Lloyd George's Ambulance Wagon*, p. 136

10 S. and B. Webb, *English Poor Law History*, part II, pp. 529-31

11 Majority Report of the Royal Commission on the Poor Laws and Relief of Distress, 1909, vol. XXXVII, p. 294, para. 220

12 ibid., p. 421, para. 604

13 ibid., p. 529, para. 10

14 Minority Report, pp. 284-5

15 Beatrice Webb, *My Apprenticeship*, p. 195

16 Minority Report, p. 405

17 ibid., pp. 670-3

18 Majority Report, p. 597, para. 4

19 S. and B. Webb, *English Poor Law Policy*, p. 302

20 S. and B. Webb, *English Poor Law History*, part II, p. 808

21 ibid., pp. 732-3

22 W. S. Churchill, *Liberalism and the Social Problem*, p. 87

4

The coming of social insurance

It was during the first forty years of the twentieth century that compulsory social insurance was generally adopted by the countries of the Western world as one of the main instruments of social policy. Voluntary social insurance had, of course, been practised by Friendly Societies and various kinds of industrial and social clubs for a very long time. Schemes of this kind were often supported by government subsidies and made to conform to regulations imposed by law to ensure their sound administration. In the case of certain classes of workers, such as miners and seamen, regulation by government was common, and Prussia had made the insurance of miners compulsory as early as 1854. But the first decisive step in the establishment of compulsory social insurance on a more general basis was taken by Bismarck in the 1880's. By 1910 it was possible for two American observers to write that 'in all countries of Europe the beginnings are readily discernible of a movement towards a complete and connected system under which working-men will be insured against all contingencies where support from wages is lost or interrupted by any cause other than voluntary cessation of labour'.[1] But, though the principle was universally accepted, it was not used in the same way by all countries, and 'complete and connected' systems did not appear everywhere quite as soon as these authors seem to have expected.

Compulsory social insurance was a novelty in three respects. It involved a new kind of interference in the affairs of industry, a new type of relationship between the citizen and the government, and new problems of finance and administration. When introduced by Bismarck it had the character of a request to industry to join with him in making concessions to meet the legitimate claims of the workers, in order to make it easier both for him and for it to resist their illegitimate ones. But as presented by an aggressive figure like

Lloyd George it had more the character of an attack, not against industrialists personally, but against the capitalist economy of the nineteenth century and against the 'establishment' which had tolerated its inhumanity. 'No one,' he said, 'can honestly defend the present system.' Side by side with great wealth there were multitudes who were not assured of even a bare subsistence. And the Liberal government aimed at something more than subsistence, namely at an income large enough to maintain efficiency for every man, woman, and child. 'The individual demands it, the State needs it, humanity cries for it, religion insists upon it.'[2] But the economy did not provide it; hence the need for the political power, backed by morality and religion, to interfere and make good the defect.

There is a curious passage in the Majority Report of the Poor Law Commission on this point. They were discussing the need for pensions, and they said: 'the evidence shows that, with very few exceptions, what working-men desire is the "cash nexus"—the bare wage contract uninfluenced by any but purely economic considerations—and the employing classes generally have accepted the situation and consider their obligations fulfilled when they pay the wage.' Most wages, they added, were fixed by collective bargaining, and the result was a 'maximum wage during the prime of life, and no wage at all when the prime is passed'.[3] They were quite right to describe the wage system in this way, but one wonders where they found the evidence that the working-men wished it to be so. It does not appear in the Appendices to their Report, and it is in conflict with what many labour leaders were saying when they denounced a system that treated labour as a commodity. But the passage brings out clearly the exact way in which compulsory insurance interfered in the affairs of industry. It inserted something into the relationship between the employer and employed which was not just the cash nexus; it interfered with the contract of employment, the very keystone of the free market economy, by writing into it a new mutual obligation. The contributions paid by and on behalf of the insured workman, and the benefits he earned thereby, became an integral part of his status as an employee.

Compulsory insurance also created a kind of contractual relationship between the insured and the State, which was a new political phenomenon. The benefits were due, as specified, because the contributions had been paid, and the government was a party to the contract, being responsilbe for its terms and for their faithful fulfilment. It was thought that this contractual element in social insurance would prevent it from becoming the plaything of party politics. Governments, out of respect for the sanctity of contract, would not feel free either to cut the benefits in the interest of economy or to increase them in a bid for votes. But in the event mass unemployment between the wars and then the fall in the value of money made constant revision of the terms of insurance necessary, affecting the rights and obligations of those already in the scheme as well as new entrants, so that hardly any subject was more constantly at the centre of political strife. It was also believed that the beneficiaries would be happy to feel that they had won their benefits by their own action (even though they had no choice in the matter), while appreciation of the fact that larger benefits must mean larger contributions would put the brake on extravagant demands.

This emphasis on the binding, contractual character of social insurance had some subtle and probably unforeseen effects. It led people to exaggerate the distinction between social insurance and social assistance, and helped to maintain the flavour of inferiority and shame that clung to the latter. Secondly it caused, or at least was accompanied by, a widespread misunderstanding of the nature of social insurance which bedevilled discussions of social policy for many years. And this brings us to the new problems of finance and administration that social insurance brought with it.

The prominence given to the term 'insurance', with all its associations of security, respectability, and virtuous providence, implied that the schemes were modelled on the current practice of insurance companies, Friendly Societies and others engaged in similar operations. But this was true only to a very limited extent even at the beginning, and it became less true as time went on, as Beveridge explained very clearly in his Report.[4]

In private insurance the income consists of the premiums paid by policy-holders and the interest on accumulated funds. The premiums are assessed in relation to the risks covered, by a process of actuarial calculation. The same terms are offered to those exposed to the same risk, but anyone whose circumstances raise the risk above the average is required to pay a higher premium. The tubercular must pay more for life insurance than the healthy, or 'good-life'. The policy-holder can, therefore, claim that he is paying the true price of the coverage he receives, and if the price seems too high, he is free to take it or leave it. With public social insurance the position is different. If the State makes insurance compulsory for a large section of the community, it has a responsibility towards the insured greater than that of a private company, just because they are not free to 'take it or leave it'. The terms enforced must be such as they can afford to meet and the benefits must bear some relation to their real needs. The only way in which they can protest against terms which they consider unfair is by political action, through Parliament; consequently the fixing of the terms is primarily a political decision and only secondarily an actuarial one. The State can accept this responsibility because it is free to diverge from the strict actuarial principles of commercial insurance. And it enjoys this freedom because it has the power to draw on money other than the subscriptions of the beneficiaries; it can compel their employers to contribute and it can transfer sums from public revenue to the insurance fund. The ultimate guarantee of the solvency of any public scheme is the power of the State to levy taxes.

There are three principal ways in which the State exercises its powers in order to give flexibility to its schemes. The first, already mentioned, is by supplementing the contributions of the insured from other sources. The second might be called the 'boosting of benefits', and the third, to use Beveridge's term, the 'pooling of risks'. The first is of general application, while the second can best be illustrated from pensions and the third from sickness and unemployment insurance.

A special position was occupied from the beginning by measures for the compensation of workmen for industrial injury, because they involve the legal liability of the employer. British law originally recognized a claim by the workman only when there was proof of negligence on the part of the employer or (by the Act of 1880) of one of his employees. But the Workmen's Compensation Act of 1897 brought British practice into line with that on the Continent of Europe by accepting the principle of 'occupational risk'. This meant that it was not necessary to prove negligence, but only that the accident arose 'out of and in the course of the employment'— since the risk was inherent in the occupation—and the principle was extended in 1906 to certain industrial diseases.

But policies differed as to the steps, if any, that the government should take to guarantee that the workman in fact received the compensation due to him. In a majority of countries this aim was achieved by making it compulsory for employers to insure their employees, at their own expense, against occupational risks, either in a central State scheme or, as in Germany, in Mutual Associations set up for the purpose by the various industries, or (exceptionally) with such insurance companies as they chose. It followed that the compensation, at standardized rates, was treated as arising not from a personal liability of the individual employer but from a social right enjoyed by the workman. In other countries, including Britain, insurance was not compulsory. It is true that most employers did insure voluntarily, but this was not insurance of the workmen against occupational risks, it was insurance of the employer against his liability to meet such claims as he could not rebut. And the workman's claim was not treated as a social right to be met out of collective funds, but as a personal claim against his individual employer which must be established by him, if necessary in a court of law. This system, which insufficiently protected the rights of the employees, persisted until after the Beveridge Report, which recommended the fusion of Workmen's Compensation with National Social Insurance.

In the case of other risks—old age, sickness, unemployment, etc. —it was the potential beneficiary who was compulsorily insured, and contributions were usually levied both on him and on his employer. In some countries social insurance was treated as being fundamentally a bipartite affair, between employer and employed, with the State only supporting the scheme from outside, as it were. Since it had set it up and made it compulsory, the least it could do was to guarantee its solvency. But it might go beyond this and contribute a lump sum annually to the funds (as in France), or add a fixed amount to each benefit paid out (as in Germany), or help to finance some special branch of the scheme which was least able to be self-supporting. But Britain, and some other countries, adopted a tripartite system in which employers, employed, and the State (or the tax-payer) are all full partners, and all make regular contributions, though not necessarily of the same amount. In British thinking this partnership was not simply an administrative convenience, but a matter of political principle, because it reflected truly the distribution of responsibility in the society.

Whatever system was adopted, it is evident that social insurance lacked the qualities that gave to private insurance its respected status as an expression of personal thrift, since the contributions of the beneficiaries were neither voluntary nor sufficient to cover the benefits. But this did not prevent people, dazzled by the magic word 'insurance', from asserting that they had a right to their benefits because they had paid for them. Or, rather less crudely, they might claim that they had paid their fair share of the price. This was true, provided that it was realized (as generally it was not) that their 'fair share' was not something that an actuary could calculate, since he could estimate only the total income needed to cover the risks. The decision as to what proportion of that total should be charged to the beneficiaries was a purely political one. The contribution of the insured person should, in fact, be regarded, not as paying for the benefits, but as qualifying him to receive them. And the State is entirely free to fix whatever qualifying conditions it may think desirable. And it has generally fixed them, for political, fiscal, and psychological reasons, in such a way as to create the appearance of some logical relationship between contributions and benefits, although in fact no such relationship exists.

In order to explain what is meant by the 'boosting of benefits' we must look at old-age pensions. Old age is not a misfortune which may fall at any time on any member of an insured population; it is a normal phase of life to which people can look forward and which they may hope to enjoy, and it comes to all, at the appointed time, provided they live long enough. So, whereas one insures against sickness or unemployment, one saves for old age, and the saving process must continue throughout one's working life. In the case of insurance against a risk, like sickness or a motor accident, what one draws out in return for a given premium depends on the extent of the damage suffered, and may be more than one had paid in; those on whom the misfortune falls benefit from the contributions of the lucky ones who escape it. And this is for the 'mutual benefit' of all, because all are equally protected against the risk. But in the case of saving for old age one can draw out, when the time comes, only what one has paid in together with the interest it has earned, and perhaps a share in the capital appreciation. And this gives rise to special problems.

First, it is difficult to persuade people to keep up their payments continuously over a long period, so there is a strong case for compulsion. Secondly, the value of money may fall and make the pension, when eventually it falls due, quite inadequate. And thirdly, when a new scheme is introduced, those who are already in middle life would, if they were allowed to join it, have to pay much larger premiums than younger men in order to earn the same pension. It is in order to overcome these difficulties that the State has so often found it necessary to 'boost the benefits' to a level above that which corresponds to the contributions made by, or on behalf of, the insured.

Voluntary insurance for old age had been practised for some time in most countries, but because of these difficulties the societies had run into trouble. In France there were so many cases of insolvency that in 1850 a ban was placed on private insurance for pensions, and public savings banks were set up instead to receive the contributions of individuals and of societies, and the State added a subvention to guarantee their stability. Belgium and Italy followed suit before the end of the century.[5] In Britain, although Gladstone had expressed alarm at the number of companies that failed and of policies that lapsed, and had established the Savings Banks and a post-office insurance scheme for the benefit of small savers,[6] no proposal was made that private savings should be subsidized by the State until Joseph Chamberlain put forward this idea in the 1890's. Its attraction for the Victorians was that the State would be helping only those who helped themselves; but it was pointed out that unfortunately the most urgent need was that of those who were far too poor to save anything at all. The suggestion was not adopted.[7]

By this time Germany had, in 1889, introduced a fully fledged scheme of compulsory contributory insurance for pensions. It covered practically all wage-earners and other employees earning less than the equivalent of £100 a year, and it provided pensions for old age (at seventy), for invalidity (i.e. permanent disability), and for widows and orphans. Employers and employees contributed equal amounts, and the State added a fixed sum to each pension. Both contributions and benefits were scaled to correspond to some extent to the level of earnings, the insured being divided for this purpose into five income classes, each with its own rates. German policy, in deciding that pensions should reflect economic inequalities, underlined the difference between insurance and assistance. In the former, the more you had the more you would receive (and also contribute), but in the latter, where a means test was used, the more you had the less you would be given.[8]

In spite of the German example, British opinion was on the whole opposed to a contributory pension scheme. The Minority Report of the Poor Law Commission had been emphatic on this point. 'The insuperable difficulties inherent in contributory schemes of Old Age Pensions', they said, had been expressed in the reports of previous Commissions 'in a manner and with an authority that we take to be conclusive'.[9] Even Bismarck himself had not intended that the employees should be obliged to contribute towards their pensions.[10] But when the Act was passed he was no longer in power, and by then all the machinery for compulsory insurance had been created to deal with sickness and accidents, and could be used for pensions. Also, since the total pension (including the State subvention) was something between 2s 6d and 3s a week, the contributions could be small.

There had been so much discussion in Britain about the needs of the aged poor that the Liberal government had to put pensions in the forefront of the programme it announced in 1906. But, argued Asquith when he introduced the Bill, it was not possible to have a contributory scheme. In the first place the administrative machinery for this did not exist. Secondly, the immediate task was to save old people from falling into the clutches of the Poor Law, and a contributory scheme could not do that, because 'none of its benefits would come into actual enjoyment until after the lapse of twenty or more years'. Till then the accumulated contribution would not be sufficient to yield a decent pension, and he did not consider the possibility of 'boosting' the benefit to make up for the deficiency. Finally a regular insurance scheme would antagonize the private agencies already engaged in the business. The government had therefore prepared a non-contributory scheme, to be financed directly out of taxes. By caring for the needs of the old in this way they would make insurance against other risks much easier. But if pensions were not to be given as an insurance benefit there must be 'some kind of discrimination' by which to select the pensioners, and the possible criteria were age, means, status, and character. The qualifying age was to be seventy. No pension at all would be paid to those whose incomes exceeded £31 10s a year, and the full pension of 5s a week would be payable only if the annual income were not more than £21. The status was that of a British subject who had not suffered imprisonment during the last ten years and was not in receipt of poor relief. And as to character, Asquith thought that the less said the better, but he was overruled and the Act stated that the pensioner must have worked to the best of his ability to maintain himself and his family.[11] In New Zealand, where a similar scheme had been introduced in 1898, the pensioner had to be 'of good character and have for five years preceding application led a sober and reputable life'.[12] These phrases reflect the anxiety lest the stigma of pauperism be lifted from those who did not deserve to be free of it—though, had they been paying something towards their pensions, the question would not have arisen. No sooner had England decided for non-contributory pensions than France, in 1910, established a contributory scheme rather like the German one. But it ran into difficulties during the war, and the State had greatly to increase its share of the cost in order to keep it solvent.

Our third point, the 'pooling or risks', is best illustrated, as we said above, by health and unemployment insurance, but it is not their most important characteristic. The outstanding fact about health insurance is that medical care is a more crucial matter than cash benefits. During the period we are considering, the concern of the State with the health of the people was being extended from the environmental to the personal services. This is in part a result of the growing sense of public responsibility for the welfare of the citizen, but there were special reasons for it as well. The evidence that was being accumulated made it clear that, although it was certainly true that bad sanitation and slum conditions were a potent cause of sickness, it was undeniable that the inadequacy of the medical services for detecting and treating illness, and for teaching people how to look after their own health and that of their children, made things worse than they need have been. If steps were to be taken to provide the cost of medical service for a large part of the population, it was essential that thought should be given to the question how that service should be organized. A start had been made in England with the school medical service, and there was a great interest in the possibility of fighting tuberculosis by individual treatment in special institutions. Professor Mackintosh has in fact claimed that 'the cause of the tuberculous was the spearhead of the campaign for a personal service at the beginning of the century'.[13] And Lloyd George, when preparing his plans for health insurance, was deeply impressed by what Germany was doing for the tubercular.[14]

At the same time the Friendly Societies and Clubs which provided medical treatment as an insurance benefit were in trouble, and this was true of many European countries. The doctors whom they employed complained that they were not paid enough, that they often had to provide the medicines themselves, and that they were being expected to treat, not only the insured persons, but their whole families, as well as many well-to-do people, who, they said, ought to come to them as private paying patients. In many places these disputes broke out into open warfare. As early as 1895 *The Lancet* had appointed a Special Commissioner to study the matter at home and abroad, and it published his reports under the general title of 'The Battle of the Clubs'. He had found not only that there was much discontent in England, but also that 'the situation across the Channel is identical with what exists in Great Britain and Ireland'.[15] In Germany the conflict continued to rage between the doctors and the Societies operating under the health insurance scheme. Each such Society negotiated its own terms of service with the association of doctors, and one of the main points of contention was the principle of the 'free choice of doctor', which the Societies were unwilling to concede. In Leipzig in 1904 mounting grievances drove the doctors to go on strike, and 'blackleg' labour of very dubious quality was brought in to take their place. After a settlement of a sort had been reached, the association of doctors closed its ranks and called on its members to 'accumulate a heavy war chest' in readiness for the next battle.[16] The German Act of 1911 did not exaggerate when it said that 'for many years keen dissensions have occurred between the doctors and the sickness insurance authorities, resulting in many places in bitter disputes and a state of open conflict'.[17]

It is perhaps not surprising that Lloyd George should have come to the conclusion that the voluntary societies must not be entrusted with the provision of medical care for the insured. But he decided to let them handle the cash benefits. Those that satisfied his conditions would be listed as 'Approved Societies' and authorized to seek the custom of those covered by the Act. The government would hand over to each Approved Society the appropriate proportion of the contributions received in respect of its clients, and the Society would undertake to pay them the statutory benefits when they fell sick. We have here an example of the 'pooling of risks' in one of its forms. It was recognized that the State, when making insurance against sickness compulsory, could not discriminate, in the terms it offered, between the sickly and the robust, or between those living in unhealthy conditions and those in healthy ones. These unequal risks must be 'pooled', even though it meant that some people would be getting what was, by strict actuarial standards, more for their money than others. But the government wanted nevertheless to preserve as much as possible of the spirit of voluntary, or commercial, insurance, and it allowed Approved Societies, if their finances permitted, to give additional benefits, such as medical appliances, dental and ophthalmic services, or extra cash. Some were able to do this, either because they were more efficiently managed than the average, or because they were extra careful in choosing their clients. They could not, of course, demand a higher premium from someone who was a 'bad risk', since the premium was fixed by law, but they could refuse to accept him. The result was that there was a considerable variation in the benefits obtained by the insured, although the contributions were the same for all.

For the general medical service the natural thing to do, one would have thought, was to entrust the organization to the local government authorities which were already in charge of Public Health, but the doctors were strongly opposed to this. Obviously they had no confidence in, or respect for, the local councillors, and that attitude has persisted. They were even more strongly against a full-time salaried service run by the government. And they insisted that the patient must be free to choose his doctor. In their anxiety about what Lloyd George might do, they threatened for a time to refuse co-operation, but the friction was largely due to the cavalier way in which he treated them during the negotiations. In principle they were with him, once he had made it clear that he accepted the three points just mentioned. So the service was organized by special Insurance Committees set up for the purpose, the patients could choose their own doctor, and the doctors who wanted to come into the scheme built up a panel of registered patients and were paid a capitation fee of so much for each patient on their register. The service was free, but it was confined to what an average general practitioner could be expected to give. It did not include specialist services, hospitalization, or dental and ophthalmic treatment.

The Bill was introduced in 1911 and Parliament received it with open arms. 'For the first few weeks', said Lloyd George, 'it was smothered in honey.' There had been nothing like it since 'the Duke of Clarence was drowned in a butt of sweet wine'.[18] But there was plenty of trouble over the details. Financially it followed the tripartite model of contributions, and its coverage was wide, embracing all wage-earners and all other employed people earning not more than £160 a year. In these respects it was generally acceptable. But it did nothing for the dependants of the insured, which was a grave blot.

Governments had been much concerned about unemployment ever since the bad days of the 1880's, but their thinking had at first been directed more to finding ways to prevent or terminate it than to measures for making up lost earnings by cash benefits; the trade unions were doing that. The attempt to cure unemployment by getting the local authorities to create work for the unemployed was admitted by everybody to have failed. And little so far had come of plans to fit the unemployed for new jobs by passing them through Training Centres, though this idea was not dead and was revived after the war. More hope was placed in the device of the Labour Bureau, which had been imported from the Continent and was showing some promise. It was one of the aims of the Unemployed Workmen Act of 1905 to establish a network of these Bureaux, or Labour Exchanges, throughout the country, but it had achieved its purpose only in the London area. Nevertheless the results were significant enough for the Majority Report of the Poor Law Commission, when drawing up recommendations on unemployment, to begin with the sentence 'in the forefront of our proposals we place labour exchanges', and the Minority agreed. In this case there is direct evidence of the influence of the Commission, because Churchill quoted this sentence when introducing the Act of 1909 which established a national system of Labour Exchanges under the direct control of the Board of Trade.[19] By 1914 they were filling just over a million vacancies,[20] but looking back on their history in 1930, William Beveridge, who had done so much to bring them into existence, found it disappointing; only one in five of the engagements of insured workpeople was made through the Exchange.[21] They were, however, key points in the administrative structure of unemployment insurance.

The system of compulsory insurance against unemployment introduced in England in 1911 was the first of its kind, apart from a disastrous experiment in a Swiss canton. Everybody knew about the 'Ghent System' by which the municipality gave annual subventions to private schemes in order to increase the benefits, and France had launched the first national system on these lines in 1905, with Norway and Denmark following suit in the next two years. But even Germany, the originator of compulsory insurance, had left unemployment out. It was not that there was any exceptional difficulty about applying the insurance principle to unemployment in normal times. On the contrary, one objection to a comprehensive State scheme was that the principle was already being applied extensively and with considerable success by the trade unions, and a State scheme might interfere with their business.

But each scheme as a rule covered only one industry or occupation, within which the risk of unemployment was of much the same kind and magnitude for all. So the principle of 'mutual benefit' could be applied. But a national scheme would have to include industries in which the risk of unemployment differed widely, and the question was how far the principle of the 'pooling of risks' could be carried. The bad risks were not, as in sickness, individual cases, but whole sections of the population to be insured. If contributions and benefits were the same for all, the stable industries would subsidize the unstable, and the efficient firms the inefficient. So the Liberal government decided to keep the inequality of risks to be covered within bounds and to start with a limited scheme confined to seven selected industries. These, as Churchill explained, were industries in which 'the unemployment is due not to a permanent contraction but to temporary oscillation in their range of business, and that is the class of business in which unemployment insurance is marked out as the scientific remedy for unemployment'.[22] Some inequality of risk did exist among these industries, but its effects were kept to a minimum by limiting the number of weeks in any one year in which benefits could be drawn, and consequently also the extent to which the contributions of one industry might be called on to pay for the unemployment in another. The scheme which was eventually embodied in Part II of the National Insurance Act of 1911 covered about two and a half million workers and was financed by contributions from employers, employees, and the State. For those not covered there remained the voluntary agencies, and the Act provided for a small subvention to be available to help these by adding one-sixth to the benefits they paid out of their funds. Beyond this there was only the Poor Law.

Such were the beginnings of compulsory social insurance, and to many people, including Winston Churchill, it marked the dawn of a new age of social policy. 'If I had to sum up the immediate future of democratic politics in a single word,' he said in 1909, 'I should say "Insurance". If I had my way I would write the word "Insure" over the door of every cottage, and upon the blotting book of every public man, because I am convinced that by sacrifices which are inconceivably small, which are all within the power of the very poorest man in regular work, families can be secured against catastrophes which would otherwise smash them up for ever.'[23] And many years later, in similar vein, he spoke of the Beveridge Report as 'bringing the magic of averages nearer to the rescue of the millions'.[24] In the first of these passages Churchill seems to be attributing to private thrift a power that is found only in public schemes, and in the second he appears to have forgotten that averages have disadvantages as well as advantages. For, as Professor Eveline Burns has well said, 'social insurance deals with *presumptive* rather than *demonstrated* need, and is a social institution dominated by a concept of *average* rather than *individual* need'.[25] When the latter exceeds the former, some method other than insurance must be used to make up the difference. The administrative device of compulsory social insurance invented at the tail-end of the age of individualism paid too little attention to the claims of the individual, and it was left to the age of mass society to remedy this defect by substituting a sufficiency for an average. And it is interesting to compare what Churchill said in 1909 with what Lloyd George jotted down on a piece of paper in 1911, when in the middle of preparing his Insurance Bill: 'Insurance necessarily temporary expedient. At no distant date hope State will acknowledge full responsibility in the matter of making provision for sickness, breakdown and unemployment.'[26]

1   L. K. Frankel and M. M. Dawson, *Workingmen's Insurance in Europe*, p. 395

2   H. du Parcq, *David Lloyd George*, vol. IV, pp. 643 and 778

3   Majority Report, p. 528, para. 2

4   Beveridge Report, p. 12, para. 24

5   A. Birnie, *Economic History of Europe*, pp. 223–4; *Provision for Old Age by Government Action in Certain European Countries*, P.P. 1899, vol. XCII

6   Dermot Morrah, *A History of Industrial Life Assurance*, pp. 29–35

7   Gertrude Williams, *The State and the Standard of Living*, pp. 67–8

8   *Provision for Old Age . . .* , pp. 14–19

9   Minority Report, p. 274

10 W. H. Dawson, *Social Insurance in Germany*, pp. 14 and 19

11 Hansard (Commons), 1908, vol. 188, cols. 466–8

12 Memorandum on Old Age Pensions (New Zealand and Germany), P.P. 1908, vol. LXXXVIII, p. 393

13 J. M. Mackintosh, *Trends of Opinion about the Public Health*, p. 33

14 W. J. Braithwaite, *Lloyd George's Ambulance Wagon*, p. 71

15 *The Lancet*, 1895, p. 476

16 I. G. Gibbon, *Medical Benefit*, pp. 27 and 236–9

17 Dawson, op. cit., p. 85

18 D. Lloyd George, *Slings and Arrows*, p. 176

19 Majority Report, p. 630; W. S. Churchill, *Liberalism and the Social Problem*, p. 254

20 S. and B. Webb, *English Poor Law History*, part II, p. 663

21 W. H. Beveridge, *Unemployment—a Problem of Industry*, p. 322

22 Frank Tillyard, *Unemployment Insurance in Great Britain*, pp. 3–4

23 Churchill, op. cit., pp. 309 and 315–16

24 W. S. Churchill, *The Second World War*, vol. IV, Appendix F, p. 862

25 E. M. Burns, *The American Social Security System*, p. 36

26 Braithwaite, op. cit., p. 121

5

The inter-war years

It is tempting to regard the twenty years that elapsed between the two world wars as an interlude dominated by desperate efforts to cope with an unprecedented depression, and to assume that when the depression ended the stream of events we have been describing resumed its course with nothing added to it but unhappy memories. But this view is untenable. It is true that the period was one not so much of great innovations as of the consolidation and expansion of measures already tested. It is true also that the guiding principles which defined the main areas of public responsibility and the rights and legitimate expectations of the citizen remained substantially the same. Nevertheless important progress took place and the scene in 1939 was very different from what it had been in 1914.

The war itself had some effect by fostering a sense of social solidarity among those who had seen it through at home and evoking a determination to offer a better life to the men returning from hellish experiences at the Front. In Britain this expressed itself in the popular slogan about 'homes fit for heroes', but the mood was short-lived. The depression which followed, striking the countries of the Western world at different moments and with differing force, also presented a challenge, to which, in some cases, the response was similar. In France the Minister introducing the comprehensive social security legislation of 1928 said that 'the essential point is that society as a whole should, in a spirit of national solidarity, assist the wage-earners to defend themselves against the dangers by which they are constantly threatened', and he repeated the word 'solidarity'.[1] In the United States the first major piece of social legislation to be passed at the Federal level went through Congress in 1935. It brought that country at one leap, not quite into line with Western Europe in the matter of social policy, but at least within talking distance. But there were also points at which the challenge was so powerful that the reaction to it was not response but collapse. This happened in the case of unemployment insurance in Britain. And elsewhere, as in the United States, although the response was positive, creative, and permanent, it was insufficient to meet the demands of the crisis, and all around it there arose a welter of temporary, emergency relief measures which happily did turn out to be no more than an interlude.

In the history of social policy wars and depressions are accidents, however important their consequences may be. But beneath the surface we can discover processes of growth which are the product of the evolutionary forces at work within social policy itself. Before the first war social reform was a political adventure run by enthusiastic amateurs; in the inter-war years social administration became a science practised by professionals. The Commissions and Committees which sat in Britain before the war, having gathered such information as they could about the past and present (and it was often fragmentary and unreliable), had little but their imagination and *a priori* reasoning to guide them when they tried to peer into the future and gauge the merits of policies which had not yet been tried. And often, as in the case of those studying the problem of the aged poor, they failed to make any recommendation at all, except that another committee should be asked to undertake further investigations. Those which met after the war were set to examine the records of systems which had been working for several years and could base their conclusions on empirical research. Typical of the first phase are the crusading fervour of Lloyd George and the hit-or-miss efforts of the little band of neophytes which he installed, with Braithwaite at their head, to design a system of health insurance under his inspiring but erratic direction. Typical of the second period are the dry matter-of-fact tones of Neville Chamberlain and the highly expert studies by William Beveridge, especially of unemployment, but also of what he called 'Insurance for All and Everything'. What strikes one about that hastily written but brilliant pamphlet is the clarity and precision of the thought, and the implied assumption that the level of understanding of the subject was by then high enough to make this very compressed picture intelligible to the general reader.

This new sophistication was a scientific not a political phenomenon. It was concerned with applying techniques, which were of universal validity, to problems that were an intrinsic part of modern industrial society wherever the income of the family was derived from the earnings of labour, and men and women fell victim to accidents and sickness. Consequently those engaged in this work used concepts and spoke a language that were not local to their home country, but international. And they could meet in conferences called by the International Labour Office (later 'Organization') and freely exchange views, pool experience, and adopt resolutions.

The result of all this was a marked convergence of social policy in all countries where social policy could be said to exist, but we must be careful not to press this point too far. We can see in the 1920's and the 1930's an emergent consensus about the nature and extent of government responsibility for social welfare. There was also general agreement as to the sections of the population to which social security legislation should apply. In addition most countries had accumulated much the same equipment of techniques and administrative machinery for use in the execution of their social policy. But here the convergence begins to weaken and is succeeded by a certain divergence of practice in deciding which instrument should be used for each particular purpose.

In some cases international convergence was the natural result of consolidation at the national level. Britain and Germany afford an example of this. Germany's first programme of social insurance included pensions and sickness but excluded unemployment; Britain's included sickness and unemployment (on a limited scale) but excluded pensions. It was natural that both countries, as they gained in experience, should fill in the gaps. Britain made unemployment insurance general in 1920 and introduced contributory pensions (at 10s. a week) in 1925; Germany added unemployment insurance to her system in 1927. After that the two systems matched very closely.

Another symptom of convergence was the movement which took place in several countries to unify their social security programmes and enclose them in a single administrative framework. France launched a composite scheme of this kind in 1928, covering sickness, maternity, invalidity, old age, and death (but not unemployment) and thus advanced at one step from a relatively backward to a quite advanced position on the social policy scale.[2] The American Social Security Act of 1935 was also a composite measure, and it has been said that Roosevelt had deliberately blocked earlier proposals of limited scope because of his 'desire to combine old-age pensions with a general program of social security and his belief that a unified program should be worked out'.[3] The Act covered pensions and unemployment, but not sickness, and it also provided Federal aid for a wide range of welfare services. But perhaps the most celebrated unified scheme is that contained in the New Zealand legislation of 1938, described by Sir Arnold Wilson as 'the most far-reaching scheme of obligatory social insurance ever included in a single enactment'. It covered old age, medical care, sickness benefit, invalidity, maternity, widows, orphans, disabled miners, unemployment, and family endowment.[4] Similar schemes of 'all-in insurance' were proposed in Britain by Beveridge, J. L. Cohen, Sir John Marriott, and others and were carefully considered by the government and rejected as impracticable.[5]

Insurance at this stage was normally confined to employed persons. It usually covered all wage-earners (except in some cases groups presenting special problems, like agricultural workers and domestic servants), and all salary-earners with incomes below a fixed maximum (except those otherwise provided for, like civil servants). This gave the impression that the whole population was now divided into two classes, those who paid and those who received. It seemed that the receipt of aid from a public service had ceased to carry the stigma of pauperism but had become an index of social class. And it raised for the first time in its modern form the issue whether social services should be used as an instrument for the redistribution of income between one class and another. Poor relief had never raised this question, since it was a kind of public charity which had no effect on society at large. But the system of social security as it had developed was a quite different affair. It was, indeed, difficult to calculate in what proportions it was returning money to those who had contributed it, transferring income on the 'mutual benefit' principle between members of the same economic class, or redistributing income from the richer to the poorer sections of the community. But it was certain that this last operation was taking place to some extent, and the question was whether it should be treated simply as the natural and inevitable consequence of services designed to satisfy real needs wherever they were found, or regarded as being an end in itself. The full-blown controversy on this point belongs to the period after the Second World War, but the situation that gave rise to it took shape during the inter-war period.

So far we have been taking note of the international convergence of social policy. When we turn to look at the techniques used in dealing with particular problems we are struck by the differences we find. In the Beveridge Report there is an Appendix that summarizes the position in 1938 in thirty countries, other than Britain, scattered over Europe, Asia, the two Americas, and Australasia. It shows that twenty had compulsory insurance against sickness, twenty-four had some form of contributory pensions, all more or less made provision for industrial injury and diseases, but only eight had compulsory unemployment insurance (not counting Germany, where it had been discontinued by the Nazis). Only three (again not counting Germany) covered all three risks of sickness, old age, and unemployment, as Britain did, and they were, rather surprisingly, New Zealand, Bulgaria, and Poland.[6] It would be quite wrong to imagine that the absence of a contributory scheme meant refusal to accept any responsibility for meeting a particular need. It indicated rather a difference of method. The responsibility towards the unemployed, for example, was frequently met by subventions to voluntary insurance supplemented by a well-developed system of social assistance, as in France. In this way the private efforts of the trade unions were stimulated, compulsion was avoided, and the objection to pooling in one scheme risks that were very unequal was met by basing the insurance on individual industries or occupations.

But arguments about principles and theories were soon overwhelmed by the catastrophic impact of the great depression and the mass unemployment that accompanied it. In Britain hardly had the decision been taken in 1920 to extend unemployment insurance to all industrial and commercial workers, in spite of the inequality of incidence of the risk, than the blow fell. By March 1921 the number of unemployed had nearly doubled, and in the 1930's the total rose perilously near to three million. In Germany the peak figure was about five million, and in the United States probably nearer ten.[7] Insurance benefits were soon exhausted, and the choice had to be made between abandoning the relationship between contributions and benefits altogether or passing the burden on to the Poor Law, that is to say on to the local rates. This was impossible, so the compromise was adopted of abandoning the principle of insurance but retaining the apparatus and as much as possible of the terminology. Relief was paid far beyond what contributions had earned by means of a succession of so-called 'transitional', 'extended', and 'uncovenanted' benefits into the nature and fortunes of which it is not necessary to go here. The result was summed up by Beveridge in 1930. Social insurance, he said, was originally contractual in character, in that it conferred a right that was conditional on the payment of contributions. Now the obligation to pay the contributions had lapsed, but the right to benefit was still acknowledged. Consequently 'the insurance scheme of 1911 has become a general system of outdoor relief to the able-bodied, administered by a national in place of a local authority, and financed mainly by a tax on employment'.[8] His mind was still ruled by the sharp antithesis between insurance and assistance, which events had so dramatically outstripped.

An heroic attempt was made in 1934 to restore the integrity of insurance. Benefits, in the true sense, were once more to be paid only in so far as contributions warranted, but a new Limbo was created in between the Heaven of insurance benefits and the Hell of poor relief over which ruled a national authority called the Unemployment Assistance Board. No stigma was to be attached to the acceptance of aid from this body but, as its payments were subject to a 'means test', which took account of the income of family members living at home, it looked just like the Poor Law under another name. Nothing in the history of social policy, except perhaps the old mixed workhouse, has inspired such hatred and detestation as this household means test. This was due partly to the inquisition necessary to make the assessment, and partly to the humiliation it caused to a man who expected to support his family, not to be supported by it. But the more fundamental cause of humiliation was the enforced idleness and the necessity to go, week after week, to draw money that had not been earned by labour. It is significant that all those in this position, whether the money they were drawing was insurance benefit or unemployment relief, were said to be 'on the dole'.

In the United States the storm broke more suddenly and was even more devastating. A vast programme of relief for the unemployed was developed, including the invention of tasks to be performed at public expense by all classes of person, including writers, scholars, and artists. But in the midst of this an attempt was made to build a permanent piece of machinery into the administrative systems of the Federal and State governments for the maintenance of the unemployed. By the Federal Act of 1935 a pay-roll tax was imposed on all industrial and commercial employers of more than seven persons, with the provision that any State which established an unemployment insurance scheme approved by the Federal government would receive the proceeds of this tax and assign them to the scheme. The practice of unemployment insurance spread gradually over the economy, but a quarter of a century later there were still fourteen million jobs not covered.[9] But the principles embodied in the legislation took root in American social policy, and it is interesting to note how closely they resemble those which Beveridge had so bitterly denounced. For the American scheme was precisely a system of 'insurance' (so-called) financed by a 'pay-roll tax' (or tax on employment) which gave the right to benefits to people by whom no contributions were payable. In the course of time, as we shall see, this conflict of principles has almost completely evaporated, and it has come to be seen that the arguments which aroused so much heat were concerned with matters of form rather than of substance.

The survey of foreign policies attached to the Beveridge Report said nothing about family allowances, because he treated them as an 'underlying assumption' of his plan, and not as an integral part of it. Their introduction in Europe was one of the most important innovations of the inter-war period. The pioneers in this adventure were France and Belgium. Voluntary systems by which wages were supplemented for the benefit of dependent children had existed for some time in both countries, and the practice was made general and compulsory by legislation in Belgium in 1930 and in France in 1932. At first this caused a divergence of policy between the countries that adopted them and those that did not. But this was a passing phase. A movement of convergence soon developed as the example set by the pioneers was generally followed, until family allowances became as common a feature of social programmes as pensions.

Family allowances differ from the other services we have so far examined in that their primary purpose is to supplement the earnings of those at work, not to maintain the income of those unable to earn. They are a means by which an individual wage is converted into a family wage by being adjusted to the number of persons who must live on it. It was natural, therefore, that these early schemes should place the whole burden of the cost on the employers. The allowances were treated as a sort of employer's liability, and the principle of insurance entered, as in the case of industrial injury, only because the employers covered their liability by sharing it among themselves. They paid a contribution proportionate to the number of their employees into an 'equalization fund' by which the allowances were financed. This destroyed any incentive there would otherwise have been to employ bachelors in preference to fathers of families.[10] One aim of the policy of family allowances was, of course, to check and if possible to reverse the fall in the birth-rate. But another, and more permanent one, was to sustain the family, as the vital nucleus of the social order. The emphasis, therefore, was on the satisfaction of need, not on the sanctity of contractual rights won by insurance contributions. In Britain the campaign led by Eleanor Rathbone on behalf of what she called the 'disinherited family' had not yet succeeded, when war broke out, in convincing the government of the merits of family allowances. Payments adjusted to family needs were an accepted feature of public assistance. It was true that they had, of dire necessity, been extended in 1921 to the unemployed in receipt of insurance benefits, but there was opposition to introducing them as a permanent feature either of the wage system or of social insurance. And when they were eventually adopted after the war, they were not placed in either of these categories, but in a special one of their own.

Meanwhile the campaign for the break-up of the Poor Law continued, both in Britain and elsewhere. The crucial question faced in all countries was, as we saw earlier, to decide whether the transfer of functions from the Poor Law authorities to other agencies could be carried to the point where the Poor Law as such would cease to exist. As far as relief in cash was concerned, its functions were being transferred to social insurance but, as we have just seen, not quite completely in the case of old people and widows and very far from completely in the case of unemployment. This movement was general. But national practices differed with regard to the services, in the fields of health, education, and welfare, which Poor Law authorities everywhere had administered for the benefit of those dependent upon them. British policy, true to the spirit of the Minority Report, aimed at their progressive absorption into the appropriate general services provided for the population at large. But these processes of transfer and absorption could not proceed freely as long as the Poor Law was administered by special authorities right outside the local government apparatus, so in 1929 the critical step was taken of abolishing the Guardians and handing over the residue of their functions to Public Assistance Committees set up by the County and County Borough Councils. The Poor Law was not abolished, but it was placed under new management with a view to its eventual disappearance.

The Act provided for the transfer of the Poor Law hospitals to the Public Health Authorities, but this happened only to a limited extent, and the Poor Law Medical Officers continued to visit and treat the poor.[11] The Public Assistance Committees also became responsible for the old people, children, feeble-minded, and others who needed institutional care, because there were no institutions to put them in except those handed over by the Guardians. We have here the germs of some of the more important modern welfare services. It was obvious that the Poor Law medical services should be taken over by specialized medical authorities of some kind, and the delay in making the transfer was due to the fact that there was, at the time, general dissatisfaction with the way the medical services were operating, but as yet no clear idea what their future structure should be. Once it was decided to set up a National Health Service, the residue of the Poor Law in this field created no problem. But there was no obvious specialized, professional authority to take over the embryo welfare services, and they remained where they were until after the war. Other Committees (Education or Public Health) might lend a hand, but the Public Assistance Committee was still responsible and it still operated under the Poor Laws. It is not easy for welfare services to shake off all association with pauperism, for they do in fact deal to a large extent with cases in which a particular misfortune is aggravated by poverty. And anybody obliged to live in a public institution at the public expense is likely to look, and to feel, like a pauper. British policy tried to achieve the transformation by means of a clean break with the past. But the replacement of the Guardians by the Public Assistance Committees was little more than the announcement of a break that could not yet be made, and British social policy suffered for some time the natural consequences of having given the dog a bad name and failed to hang it. The reputation of the Poor Law was blackened, but it was not killed, and it continued to leave its mark on everything it touched. Eventually, as we shall see, the policy succeeded, to the point of creating welfare services to which poverty was an irrelevant circumstance; but it got there the hard way, by wiping out the past and starting afresh.

Other countries pursued a different course. They did not condemn the Poor Law to death by dismemberment, but tried to humanize and modernize it. In France and Germany, for instance, public assistance continued to function as a multi-purpose service meeting all the needs of the very poor, who were treated as a distinct category, but one which should become smaller as social security measures became more comprehensive. The French *aide sociale* and the German *Fürsorge* provided not only maintenance of all kinds, but help in paying rents, medical and maternity services at home or in hospital (with choice of doctor), education, and vocational training of the handicapped. Thus, while the destitute were set apart from the rest of the population, it was intended that they should be served in the same spirit as the others, an ideal that could not always be realized.[12] In Scandinavia a rather similar development took place, which has been described as 'the transformation of poor relief into modern social assistance'. The sharp separation of the category of the very poor from the rest of the community seems to have been absent, and it was possible to bring under one authority the idle and obstreperous poor, who needed to be subjected to deterrent discipline, those whose main trouble was extreme poverty, and those for whom poverty was only a subsidiary factor in a situation dominated by some misfortune or affliction.[13]

In the United States public assistance, which had been modelled on the English Poor Law, was indeed broken up, but mainly by a process of internal specialization rather than transfer to the general public services. In the nineteenth century the practice had grown up of giving 'preferential assistance' to specially deserving cases; such assistance was both more generous than the average and was supposed to carry no stigma of pauperism. Several States then started special programmes for selected classes of persons—mothers of young children, the aged, and the blind. This so-called 'categorical assistance' spread slowly and was attacked as unconstitutional on the grounds that it involved the 'payment of public funds to persons who were not in need'. In a sense this was true, and it did imply a radical departure from traditional Poor Law principles. The Social Security Act of 1935 standardized the system by offering Federal aid for schemes on behalf of the old, dependent children, the blind, and the permanently disabled, while recognizing, but not aiding, a fifth category of 'general assistance', which was the old Poor Law under a new name. Thus the area of public assistance was expanded, both as regards the needs provided for and the population covered, but it remained 'assistance', in that the services were non-contributory and the benefits were granted subject to a means test.[14] But these measures did much to change the harsh spirit of what Edith Abbott called 'our un-American American Poor Laws'.[15]

If family allowances were the most important practical innovation in social policy during the inter-war years, housing was the most important item to be added to the list of things with which social policy had to deal. Speaking of Britain before the First World War

Dr Marian Bowley says that at that time 'the housing problem was the slum problem, the problem of people living in insanitary conditions'.[16] It is true that the main emphasis had been on housing as a branch of Public Health, but the idea that government, both central and local, had some responsibility for what another writer on the subject calls 'house building as distinct from slum clearance' had been translated into legislation in 1890 and 1909, and the distinction was reflected in the regulations governing the two operations. But, although 'housing became a burning question of municipal politics', very little was done to provide houses outside the slum-clearance areas.[17]

The war gave to the housing question a new urgency. Building had been suspended, and rents had been frozen in order to prevent the exploitation of the housing shortage. And the men at the Front had been promised 'homes fit for heroes' on their return. It would hardly have been tactful to greet them with a big rise in rents, and yet, at the level at which they then stood, there was no incentive to private firms to build houses to let to working-class families. And people were beginning to regard their controlled rents as representing the true value of their houses. It was in these circumstances that British housing policy first appeared in the guise of a social service. The responsibility for coping with the crisis was placed firmly on the local authorities; they were to make surveys and prepare plans to meet the needs that they revealed. They were to let the houses they built at rents which bore no necessary relation to their cost, but were assessed in the first instance by reference to the controlled rents for similar accommodation in old houses, and then adjusted to the tenant's capacity to pay. Any loss suffered on the transaction in excess of the yield of a rate of one penny in the pound would be made good by the Exchequer. Under a scheme of this kind both the local authorities and their tenants would receive aid in proportion to their needs. But this policy, which set no limit to what the local authorities could spend, proved too costly, and also failed to deliver the goods, and was abandoned in 1923. Thereafter the subsidies paid by the Exchequer to the local authorities were limited to fixed amounts, and the trend, if we ignore the oscillations of policy associated with changes of government, was towards relying mainly on private enterprise for new building, while concentrating public expenditure on special tasks, such as slum-clearance and the reduction of overcrowding. At the same time attempts were made to bring rent restriction to an end by gradually lowering the maximum value of houses whose rents remained controlled, but the operation was never completed, and at the outbreak of the war about one quarter of the rents were still controlled.[18]

The experience of the other European countries that had been involved in the war was very similar. Some of them had started to evolve a housing policy, and the machinery with which to implement it, even before the war. France in particular had, by 1906, developed the whole apparatus of public loans, cheap land, guaranteed interest, and tax relief to help Housing Societies to build houses and let them to working-class families at rents which they could afford.[19] Between the wars there was a convergence of policy in Europe, in the sense that all countries took steps to control rents and stimulate building, but they differed as to the extent to which they subsidized rents. In Scandinavia rents rose as much as the cost of food, but in France, Germany, and Italy considerably less. European policy also differed in certain points from British. There was less inclination to adjust individual rents to incomes than to adjust incomes to rent; they preferred, as Alva Myrdal says of Sweden, to subsidize families rather than houses.[20] More use, on the whole, was made of tax remission as an encouragement to build, perhaps because there were more taxes that could conveniently be remitted, especially taxes on land. But most significant was the multiplication of housing associations, co-operatives, and semi-official, autonomous institutions for financing the building of houses on a non-profit basis. The methods varied but the purpose was the same, namely to provide dwellings which could be let at moderate rents to families with incomes below a certain fixed level, with the minimum of administrative intervention by the local authorities.[21]

The inter-war years saw, finally, two developments of lasting importance which affected the whole character of social policy. The depression, and above all its devastating effects in the areas most heavily hit by it, caused the whole picture of social problems to change. It was realized that social policy must be conceived as a part of general economic policy, and not as a separate area of political action governed by principles peculiar to itself. The vital necessity was to restore the volume of employment, and the relief of the unemployed was a subsidiary matter. In fact, care had to be taken to see that relief was not administered in such a way as to discourage efforts to end the slump. Thus the way was prepared for the Beveridge doctrine that there could be no effective system of social security without a policy of full employment.

In what came to be known as the 'Special Areas' the task confronting the authorities was nothing less than the rescue of community life in all its forms. Efforts were made to set up new industries, to organize emigration, to devise 'sub-economic' occupations and provide land for 'subsistence production' by which men could be given something to do and could earn a small profit without sacrificing their status as unemployed, and it was equally essential to offer entertainment, recreation, and ways of using leisure which might stimulate the faculties and engage the attention of men and youths condemned to idleness.[22]

The second important development was in the role of the voluntary societies. It was probably in the nineteenth century that the boldest and most imaginative pioneering work was done by private individuals, after which there came a period when some of the leading voluntary organizations were associated with reactionary and conservative views, while the public services embarked on new enterprises, often following a lead that had been given them by the most effective private individuals and agencies. In the inter-war period the pioneering role of voluntary societies was once more conspicuous, while new forces began to stir in some of the older and more conservative bodies. But this time the public and private sectors advanced together so closely and in such harmony that the characteristic feature of the age was partnership between the two. In the early years of the century, says Mr Bourdillon, the question was whether a service should be voluntary or statutory, but by the end of the thirties the answer clearly was that both were needed, and the problem was 'not whether to co-operate but how to co-operate'.[23]

Many examples could be given. Public services for maternity and child welfare began to be systematically developed on the basis of two Acts of Parliament. The first, in 1915, made it compulsory for the doctor or midwife to notify every birth within thirty-six hours. This gave an infinitely better basis of information for health visitors than the obligation on parents to register the birth, which had existed since 1874. Secondly, the Maternity and Child Welfare Act of 1918 authorized and encouraged local authorities to develop services for expectant and nursing mothers and for children under five. In this large field, which included health visiting, maternity and child welfare clinics, children's homes, nursery schools, and day nurseries, the voluntary and statutory agencies went forward side by side and hand in hand. The Blind Persons Act of 1920 empowered local authorities to carry out the duties imposed upon them through the medium of voluntary agencies, and this was extensively done.[24] Voluntary youth organizations had existed since the middle of the last century, but it was only in 1916 that the government made its first attempt to set up central and local machinery to co-ordinate the whole range of voluntary and statutory activities, recreational and educational, that were concerned with youth.

One of the most significant developments in this period was the creation of the National Council of Social Service, and the supporting regional or local councils, with the task of smoothing the way to co-operation between voluntary bodies of all kinds, and between them and the public authorities. It was primarily, said G. D. H. Cole, 'not a charitable agency, but a fosterer and co-ordinator of communal activities among ordinary people, and not merely among the "poor" in any narrow sense'.[25] It was the moving spirit behind the drive to establish local Community Centres run on democratic principles by Community Associations which attracted so much attention and aroused such high hopes in the years immediately before the Second World War. It was felt that this represented the vital change from services offered and institutions created by benevolent outsiders, to reliance on self-help and mutual aid. And the National Council also dispensed about a million pounds of government money for the foundation and management of 'occupational clubs' for the unemployed in the depressed areas.

Little or nothing has been said in this chapter about the health services. Had the story been told here it would have consisted largely of growing evidence of dissatisfaction with the state of affairs and tentative proposals for reforms and additions, on which no action was taken. It is more convenient to treat of these matters in the next chapter.

1   C. W. Pipkin, *Social Politics and Modern Democracies*, vol II, p. 196
2   ibid., pp. 202–5
3   Paul Douglas, *Social Security in the United States*, p. 11
4   Arnold Wilson and G. S. Mackay, *Old Age Pensions*, p. 203
5   ibid., pp. 88–9
6   Beveridge Report, Appendix F, p. 287
7   R. C. Davison, *British Unemployment Policy since 1930*, pp. 111 and 128
8   W. H. Beveridge, *Unemployment—a Problem of Industry*, 1930, pp. 288–9

 9 Douglas, op. cit., pp. 12 and 130; *The Social Welfare Forum*, 1962, p. 9

10 D. V. Glass, *Population Policies and Movements*, chapter 3

11 Norman Wilson, *Municipal Health Services*, pp. 87–99

12 André Rouast et Paul Durand, *Sécurité sociale*, pp. 473–505; Heinrich Braun, *Industrialization and Social Policy in Germany*, p. 90

13 George P. Nelson (ed.), *Freedom and Welfare*, pp. 446–60

14 Hilary M. Leyenbecker, *Problems and Policies of Public Assistance*, pp. 52–5 and 82–5

15 Edith Abbott, *Public Assistance*, vol. I, p. 125

16 Marian Bowley, *Housing and the State 1919–1944*, p. 3

17 G. Slater, *Poverty and the State*, pp. 243–8

18 Bowley, op. cit., *passim*; John Greve, *The Housing Problem*, p. 11

19 Pipkin, op. cit., vol. II, pp. 156–7

20 Alva Myrdal, *Nation and Family*, p. 242

21 ILO, *Housing Policy in Europe*, 1930, *passim*

22 Davison, op. cit., chapter 5

23 A. C. F. Bourdillon, *Voluntary Social Services*, p. 164

24 ibid., p. 57

25 ibid., p. 26

6

The war and the Welfare State

A modern total war has certain predictable effects on the social problems of the warring nations. It absorbs the unemployed, it stimulates health services in both their technical and their organizational aspects, and it creates a housing shortage, either by destroying houses or preventing them from being built, or both. In a more general sense total war obliges governments to assume new and heavier responsibilities for the welfare of their peoples, especially by controlling the production and distribution of scarce necessities, like food and fuel, and by looking after those who have been made homeless by invasion, evacuation, or aerial bombardment. The experience of total war is therefore bound to have an effect on both the principles of social policy and the methods of social administration. But the nature of this effect will depend to a considerable extent on the fortunes of war—on whether a country is invaded or not, on whether it is victorious or defeated, and on the amount of physical destruction and social disorganization it suffers.

Britain's experience in the war was unique. It was the only sovereign state that fought right through from the beginning to the end, enduring attacks on the homeland but not invasion, and finally emerged victorious, without having at any time suffered social or political disorganization. These circumstances help to explain why the concept of the Welfare State first took shape in England. The magnitude of her war effort and her vulnerability to attack called for sacrifices from all and equally for help given ungrudgingly and without discrimination to all who were in need. 'The pooling of national resources', says Professor Titmuss, 'and the sharing of risks were not always practicable nor always applied; but they were the guiding principles.'[1] And the political stability of the country, combined with its unshaken confidence in victory, account for the most remarkable feature of the story, namely the way in which the people and their government, in the middle of the war, set about drawing the designs of the new society which was to be born when the fighting stopped. It was to be a society governed by the same principles of pooling and sharing that governed the emergency measures of the war. So the idea of the Welfare State came to be identified with the war aims of a nation fighting for its life. It is not surprising that, in England, it wore a halo which is not to be found in other countries when, in due course, they undertook the task of social reconstruction. And it is not surprising that, when it came to be examined in detail, with the cold eye of reason, its more fervent champions strapped on their armour and declared a holy war on its critics.

As early as 1941 the Ministry of Health announced as 'the objective of the Government, as soon as may be after the war', the creation of a comprehensive hospital service available to all.[2] In 1943 the Board of Education published a report of the Youth Advisory Council (set up for this purpose in 1942) on 'The Youth Service after the War'. In 1944 Parliament passed an Education Act which was intended to give full equality of opportunity to all, regardless of family income, and the government published its plan for a National Health Service. But the boldest attempt to set down on paper the nation's peace aims in terms of a new social order was the Beveridge Report of 1942. The government had already committed itself, through the mouth of Anthony Eden, to the principle that 'social security must be the first object of our domestic policy after the war',[3] and had insisted on writing 'social security, into the Atlantic Charter. So Beveridge was fully justified in saying' at the end of his Report, that 'statement of a reconstruction policy by a nation at war is statement of the uses to which that nation means to put victory, when victory is achieved'.[4] And it was as a blueprint of the social order for which the country was fighting that the Report was received and acclaimed.

And yet, when one reads it, one finds that it was in the main, as the government had intended it to be, a technical analysis of the problems and methods of social insurance, with some drastic and often very ingenious proposals for unifying the whole system and making it simpler and more efficient. In these respects it is a remarkable document which had a deep effect on social policy not only in Britain but in other countries as well. But this alone cannot account for its immense popular appeal. There was, in fact, in the social insurance plan itself only one really arresting innovation, namely the extension of the compulsory insurance scheme to include the entire population. But the main cause of the enthusiastic reception of the Report was no doubt the picture it drew—or in parts merely sketched—of the total social programme of which the Beveridge plan proper was only a part. The Report expressed a great idea and presented a grand design which seemed to proclaim a social revolution. In a famous and much-quoted passage Beveridge declared that social insurance was indeed 'an attack upon Want. But Want is only one of the five giants on the road of reconstruction and in some ways the easiest to attack. The others are Disease, Ignorance, Squalor and Idleness.'[5] His Plan for Social Security was a plan to abolish Want, but it could only succeed if the other giants were attacked at the same time. So he listed three assumptions which underlay his proposals, namely that provision would be made for allowances for dependent children, for comprehensive health and rehabilitation services, and for the maintenance of employment.[6] And he might have added, with an eye to the two giants Ignorance and Squalor, education and houses for the people.

Did all this amount to a social revolution? Beveridge himself answered this question. 'The scheme proposed here', he wrote, 'is in some ways a revolution, but in more important ways it is a natural development from the past. It is a British revolution.'[7] This is true. For what we see here is the final phase in the process described in the second chapter of this book, by which the logical development and natural evolution of ideas and institutions led ultimately to a transformation of the system. The transformation, or revolution, consisted in the welding together of the measures of social policy into a whole which, for the first time, acquired thereby a personality of its own and a meaning that had hitherto been only vaguely glimpsed. We adopt the term 'Welfare State' to denote this new entity composed of old elements. The total ultimate responsibility of the State for the welfare of its people was recognized more explicitly than ever before, and the choice between the three political philosophies described in Chapter 2 was clearly decided. The social services were not to be regarded as regrettable necessities to be retained only until the capitalist system had been reformed or socialized; they were a permanent and even a glorious part of the social system itself. They were something to be proud of, not to apologize for. But even here there were reservations. When the National Government presented (in 1944) its version of the Beveridge plan of social insurance, it prefaced it with a statement which contained a tactful warning. National policy, it said, must aim to

secure 'the general prosperity and happiness of the citizens. To
realize that aim two courses of action must be followed. The first
is to foster the growth of the national power to produce and to
earn, with its accompanying opportunities for increased well-being,
leisure and recreation. The second is to plan for the prevention of
individual poverty resulting from those hazards of personal fortune
over which individuals have little or no control.'[8] The government
was anxious not to spread the idea that social security is a substitute for productivity, but it was referring at this point to social
insurance only, and not to the whole programme of the Welfare
State. Education and health may well be regarded as contributing
more to the increase of productivity than to the prevention of
poverty.

Beveridge set himself the task of consolidating the various social
insurance schemes, standardizing the benefits, where appropriate,
and adding new benefits where necessary so as to cover all needs
caused by loss of income, or the incidence of exceptional demands
upon income, such as those arising from marriage and death. He
proposed to bring Workmen's Compensation (or Industrial Injury)
within the scope of social insurance so that compensation would be
received as a benefit, instead of having to be claimed from the
employer, if necessary in a court of law. This was done. He proposed
to convert old-age pensions into retirement pensions, payable only
when the claimant gave up regular work. Those who preferred to
go on working, and contributing, beyond the minimum age of
sixty-five for men and sixty for women would receive proportionately larger pensions when they retired. This was also done. Next,
he proposed to fill the two most serious gaps in the pre-war benefits.
Allowances for dependants were given only to widows and the unemployed, not to pensioners and the sick. Beveridge insisted that
all benefits should include all members of the family, unless they
were otherwise provided for. And he wanted husband and wife to
receive a 'joint benefit', so as not to insult a wife by calling her a
'dependant'. This typical touch was ignored. Secondly, unemployment benefit was limited to a maximum number of weeks in each
year. He wished to pay it without time limit, subject to the condition
that, after a certain period, the unemployed man must attend a
training centre. This bold proposal, showing great confidence in
the possibility of maintaining full employment, was rejected.

Of the new benefits proposed the most important was children's
(or family) allowances, beginning with the second child. The case

for these had long been unsuccessfully urged, and it had now become clear that one could not refuse to do for the employed what had already been done for the unemployed, or the latter might sometimes find themselves better off than the former. The allowances, though an essential element in the total plan, were not be to given as an insurance benefit, but financed out of taxes. Of the six other new benefits recommended by Beveridge, only two were eventually accepted, maternity and funeral grants. His idea of adding a grant for marriage, benefits for deserted wives, home helps for sick housewives, and training grants for the self-employed were either too ingenious or too complicated to win political support. Home helps did indeed materialize, but as part of the local welfare service.

But our main concern here is not with the details but with the basic principles of the Beveridge Report, and on this subject its author was quite explicit. We can group them under three heads. First, the plan must be one of universal, compulsory, and contributory insurance. Secondly, contributions and benefits must be at the same flat rate for all, the benefits being fixed at subsistence level. And, thirdly, statutory benefits should be supplemented by voluntary saving, which should be encouraged by positive measures included in this scheme. These three principles are interlocked and interdependent.

Universal coverage was the boldest innovation in the Beveridge plan. And yet, although he admitted that the only two countries which had adopted it were New Zealand and the Soviet Union and that in neither of these was the scheme one of genuine insurance, he had little to say in defence of his departure from generally accepted practice. He seemed to assume that, given the spirit of the times, it was inevitable. And so, perhaps, it was, but it had its critics, of whom one of the most vehement and effective was the economist H. D. Henderson. He declared that the extension of compulsory insurance to the middle classes could not possibly do anything to further Beveridge's 'proclaimed objective of abolishing want'. The logical way to do this was to locate and measure the want and to raise and dispense enough money to relieve it.[9]

But Beveridge could not consider this for a moment, because it was not insurance. It resembled the New Zealand scheme, which was later described by one of its administrators as one in which 'each citizen would contribute according to his means, and from which he could draw according to his need'.[10] And that was public assistance

financed by a tax. The essence of insurance was the interdepend-
ence of contributions and benefits, and it was contributory insurance, so he believed, that the people of England wanted. They
wanted it as the only alternative to the hated 'means test' of the
inter-war years. His aim, therefore, was 'to ensure at all times to all
men a subsistence income for themselves and their families as of
right; that is to say without any form of means test or enquiry
about other means they had'.[11]

In stressing the idea that benefits must be granted 'as of right' he
was, of course, expressing correctly the central aim of European
social policy since the beginning of the century. It had been inter-
nationally endorsed in 1925 when an ILO Conference resolved
that social security for the workers 'can best be attained by means
of a system of social insurance granting clearly defined rights to
the beneficiaries'.[12] But it did not follow that these rights could be
established only by contributions. Beveridge had himself argued,
in his book *Insurance for All and Everything*, that insurance is simply
the 'collective bearing of risks', irrespective of the source from
which the insurance fund derives its income. A scheme ceases to
rank as social insurance only when 'the receipt of the benefit depends
in any way upon the discretion of some authority'.[13] And a French
Deputy went still further and maintained that social differs from
commercial insurance precisely because the worker 'is insured not
by personal contribution but by society, which gives him rights and
guarantees them in the prevention, relief, and compensation against
loss arising out of social risks'.[14] That is the point; it is society that
gives the rights, and it may attach them to contributions or not,
as it pleases.

But, although he insisted on the contractual character of contributory insurance, Beveridge recognized, and clearly explained,
the differences between social and other forms of insurance. In
social insurance, he said, there can be a 'pooling of risks'. We have
already seen how this worked for sickness and unemployment,
where in each case risks of the same kind but of different degree
were covered by equal contributions. In devising a comprehensive
plan in which a single contribution on one card covered all benefits,
he extended the 'pooling' over the whole field and over risks of
different kinds. Secondly, although contributions must be related
to benefits, the relationship could, he said, be whatever seemed
desirable on general grounds; it need not be based on actuarial calculations. The contributions should 'be high enough to give the

insured person, because he has contributed substantially without reference to means, a justifiable claim to receive benefit without reference to means'.[15] But what level of contributions that indicates is anybody's guess.

There are also grounds for questioning, or amending, Beveridge's sharp distinction between a benefit received 'as of right' and one that is subject to a 'means test', or dependent 'upon the discretion of some authority'. For the means 'test', as used between the wars, was not really discretionary. The benefit was adjusted to the family income by a fixed scale; there was inquisition (which was resented), but not discretion. For discretion enters only when one begins to assess needs. Means can be measured by rule of thumb and arranged along a scale, but needs cannot, because each case is unique. A means test is an appropriate instrument for assessing what somebody should pay for a service, like a university education, but not for assessing what somebody, who *ex hypothesi* is on the verge of destitution, ought to receive. In such cases it is liable to be used to check extravagance and to detect malingering. What is really required is a 'needs test', which, in the broadest sense of the term, is the foundation of every benevolent welfare service.

Beveridge's second principle, of the flat rate and the subsistence level, was also, as he well knew, one that few other governments favoured. 'In most other countries', he wrote, 'the benefits are percentages of the wages, and vary, therefore, from one man to another.'[16] Here we see most clearly the influence of his political philosophy, the philosophy of twentieth-century Liberalism. The State, he argued, was entitled to compel people to contribute to the cost of guaranteeing for themselves the absolute minimum income necessary for subsistence. There was no room here for individual preferences in expenditure. But 'to give by compulsory insurance more than is needed for subsistence is an unnecessary interference with individual responsibilities'. He called this 'the principle of a national minimum, above which all citizens shall spend their money freely'.[17] Subsistence benefits must be flat-rate benefits, for the subsistence level, however you calculate it, is an absolute, and not a relative, quantity of income. And, if the principle of contributory insurance is to be adhered to, flat-rate benefits imply flat-rate contributions. In so far as it was desirable to depart from this principle and transfer income from the richer to the poorer, this should be done through that part of the total cost which is met out of the proceeds of progressive taxation. That is why Beveridge favoured the 'tri-partite' system in which employers, employed, and tax-payers all contribute, and decided to increase the share of the tax-payers.

'Subsistence' was for Beveridge both an advance on the past and a limitation on the future. In the inter-war years benefits were not meant to provide a living, but merely a substantial supplement to other resources. Subsistence in Beveridge's plan meant an adequate income, even when there were no other resources at all. He envisaged a National Assistance service, centrally administered, to take over the functions of the old Poor Law with respect to outdoor cash relief, but it was basic to his plan that nobody should have to ask for National Assistance simply because his insurance benefits were inadequate. National Assistance would be chiefly concerned with caring for the anomalies, including those who, whether by their own fault or not, were not qualified to receive benefit. It would give relief, subject to a means test, and it 'must be felt to be something less desirable than insurance benefit; otherwise the insured people get nothing for their contributions'.[18]

Could such a scheme really work? The subsistence level of Beveridge looked suspiciously like the 'poverty line' of Rowntree, and the calculations on which the former was based owe much to those used for the latter. But whereas Rowntree's 'poverty line' was an instrument of social research which could, in accordance with the definition of a 'line', be without breadth, the subsistence level was an operational concept which must provide a margin of safety and some room for manœuvre in a changing world. When the value of money steadily falls and prices rise erratically and unevenly from place to place and commodity to commodity, a universal subsistence benefit becomes unworkable. And if the benefit is raised for all above the danger point, the flat-rate contributions which correspond to the new level become higher than the poorest members of the society can afford. It was on these grounds that the National Government, in its White Paper of September 1944, explicitly rejected Beveridge's proposal. It would, they said, mean tying the benefit to the cost of living, and either varying benefits according to individual needs (which is not insurance), or raising contributions to an impossibly high level.[19] The scheme later introduced by the Labour government aimed at subsistence but did not achieve it, for the government was driven more and more to supplement the benefits of those who had no private means by allowances from National Assistance. For this they were denounced by Beveridge in the House of Lords, who called on them either to raise the benefits or to state 'that they formally abandon security against want without a means test and declare that they drop the Beveridge Report and the policy of 1946'.[20]

On that occasion Beveridge was defending his beloved child, and he may be forgiven for passing lightly over its possible defects. But did he, when making subsistence the guiding principle of his plan, foresee the difficulties it would encounter? In one respect he certainly did, for he discussed it at some length. This was the matter of rents. Rents vary from place to place and may represent a large item of expenditure in small budgets. And it is not always possible to reduce the expenditure by moving to a cheaper home. Could a uniform subsistence benefit absorb this item? In the case of National Assistance it was found that it could not, and the practice was followed of fixing the standard allowance exclusive of rent, and adding what was needed to pay the rent afterwards. Beveridge carefully considered arrangements of this kind and rejected them as inconsistent with his basic principles. His whole attitude to this question, and to the problem of rising prices, now seems to have been short-sighted. Perhaps he anticipated more effective measures to check inflation than were actually adopted. And undoubtedly he relied very much on his hope that most people would add to the statutory benefits by voluntary insurance.

And this brings us to the third of his major principles, the importance of leaving room for private saving. He wanted positive steps to be taken to encourage this. He had two suggestions to make, put forward, not as integral parts of the plan, but as 'eminently desirable'. He had decided against continuing to use 'Approved Societies' to operate sickness insurance as independent agents because of the inequality of benefits that resulted. But he wanted them to act as channels through which standard, statutory benefits were distributed, so as to give them an opportunity to persuade people to take out additional policies voluntarily. He did not include in this proposal the commercially run Industrial Assurance, or 'Collecting', Societies, because, as he said, they were run for profit. And he proposed that their business should be taken over by a national Board, having a monopoly of this kind of business, conferred by statute. Neither of these proposals was adopted.

As a result, the balance of the plan was upset. Beveridge spoke of it as 'combining three distinct methods: social insurance for basic needs; national assistance for special cases; voluntary insurance for additions to the basic provision'.[21] The third of these methods was left to take care of itself, but action was taken to institute the second. The Act of 1948, which set up the National Assistance Board, opened with the words (already quoted in an earlier chapter) 'the existing poor law shall cease to have effect'. The clean break with the past was made at last, and it involved two important innovations which distinguish the British from most other systems. First, relief in cash was shifted from the rates to the taxes, that is to say, from the local authorities to a national body. The ancient tradition of the Western world that the relief of the poor is the affair of their neighbours was brought to an end. Secondly, cash benefits were, as a result, sharply separated from personal services. These, apart from the over-all responsibility to provide shelter for vagrants, were entrusted to local councils. The way was open for the development of modern welfare services, offered to all who needed them and free from any flavour of charity or taint of pauperism. But the taint remained obstinately clinging to the National Assistance Board. Should we say that it was sacrificed in order that the welfare services might be born free of original sin? Or would it have been possible, if the two services had remained together, to purify both of them? No definite answer can be given to these questions, but the experience of the Scandinavian countries suggests that the second might be nearer the truth.

The second main supporting pillar of the Welfare State was the National Health Service. When the Labour government introduced the Bill which became the Act of 1946, its spokesman stressed the fact that it was the 'outcome of a concerted effort extending over a long period of years', and achieved what responsible people had been advocating since before the war. Nor was it 'the preserve of any one party'.[22] This was perfectly true, but it cannot be too strongly emphasized that a National Health Service is something essentially different from a system of health insurance. The survey made for the Royal Commission of 1924–6 of fourteen foreign countries showed that medical care was treated in all of them as an insurance benefit, as it was in Britain. In some countries the schemes were still voluntary, but there were clear signs of a trend towards the introduction of compulsory schemes covering specified classes of the population, again as in Britain. Most of them were administered by local bodies—either 'approved societies' or semi-autonomous statutory bodies representing the locality. These negotiated with the local doctors and made arrangements with the local hospitals and clinics for the medical care of their clients, the insured families. They tried to cover as many types of treatment as possible, and they generally offered at least some of them to dependants. Patients usually had to pay part of the cost of the treatment they received. If a system of this kind worked smoothly it meant that some attempt could be made to plan the use of the local resources to the best advantage, and that no commercial transaction took place between the patient and his doctor. But the service was entangled in all the complexities of contributory insurance, and was available only to those who were qualified to receive it by fulfilment of the terms of the insurance contract. And there was no overall plan for the distribution of medical resources throughout the country, or for their systematic development. And, as we saw earlier, systems of this kind did not always work smoothly, and one way of avoiding friction between the local agencies and the medical profession was to refrain from providing services free (or nearly free) to those entitled to receive them, and instead of this to reimburse in cash the cost (or part of it) of the treatment the patient had managed to obtain for himself. This happened extensively in Germany and as the general rule in France, and represents the furthest remove of an insurance system from anything that could be called a health service.

The pre-war British system was a compromise. General practice by 'panel doctors' had something of the character of a national service, and it was claimed that the distribution of practitioners in relation to population had greatly improved, as well as the quality of the service provided.[23] But there was no local authority to coordinate the medical services; hospitals, general practice and public health were separately administered. And, as in Europe, the operation of the whole machine was clogged by the paraphernalia of insurance. This can be illustrated by a few random quotations from a description written during the war. 'The inside of an Insurance Committee's building is a gigantic filing system . . . Every insured person is indexed both according to his doctor and according to his Approved Society . . . Changes of doctor give endless trouble to the staff . . . The scheme suffers because it is geared to the obsolescent organization of general practice in this country . . . The trouble with the National Health Insurance is that it is not "national". Administrative emphasis is on the word "insurance". The sick are considered not as citizens but as insured persons.'[24]

The case for a planned national health service was foreshadowed by two Reports published between the wars. The first, the so-called

'Dawson Report', was prepared by the Consultative Council set up
to advise the government. It approached the subject from a strictly
practical and professional angle, and not with any preconceived
theories about the principles of social policy. 'The changes that we
advise', it said, 'are rendered necessary because the organization of
medicine has become insufficient, and because it fails to bring the
advantages of medical knowledge adequately within reach of the
people.'[25] The general practitioner was cut off from modern facilities
for diagnosis and treatment and from contact with specialists and
consultants. To remedy this the Report proposed to set up Health
Centres at two levels, local ones as bases for the general practitioners, and regional ones for specialists. The latter, it seems, would
in fact be miniature hospitals. The existing voluntary hospitals,
which had 'fallen on evil days', were to be resuscitated and worked
into a general service directed by local health authorities. The Royal
Commission of 1924–6 saw things in much the same light, and had
visions of a comprehensive medical service. 'The ultimate solution
will lie', they said, 'in the direction of divorcing the medical service
entirely from the insurance system and recognizing it along with
all the other public health activities as a service to be supported
from the general public funds.'[26] But the time, they thought,
was not ripe. In view of the mounting burden of public expenditure, 'the State may justifiably turn from searching its
conscience to exploring its purse'.[27] So nothing of importance was
done.

But the war conquered these inhibitions, and the Beveridge
Report paved the way for action. It is interesting to compare the
plan put forward by the National Government with the Act passed
under the Labour government. The former left the hospitals much
as they were, but created new Joint Authorities, formed by amal-
gamating contiguous local government areas, to run the rest of the
services. The aim was to rehabilitate and reintegrate general practice,
and make it the backbone of the service, which was what all the
inter-war experts had recommended. But the doctors were alarmed.
They saw this as the first step towards converting them into 'a
service of technicians controlled by central bureaucrats and by
local men and women entirely ignorant of medical matters'.[28]
Aneurin Bevan, for the Labour government, turned this plan up-
side down. He left the general practitioners much as they were,
except that the old Insurance Committees were replaced by Executive Councils half of whose members represented the professions,

and new and far more effective means were devised for controlling the distribution of practices. But he took the drastic step of nationalizing the voluntary hospitals and putting them, and the municipal hospitals, all under Boards appointed by, and responsible to, himself. The teaching hospitals had each its own governing body directly under the Minister, while the rest were grouped geographically under Regional Boards. And, in due course, it became clear that the hospitals had become the backbone of the service, while general practice struggled along in a state of intermittent dissatisfaction both with its remuneration and with the conditions under which it had to work. An optimistic general practitioner wrote in 1949, having described what was then wrong with the service: 'The new order of things may alter this. The liaison between health centres and hospitals, the idea of general practitioner hospitals, the growing feeling that it is absurd to train students in modern methods and then to deny them the use of these methods when they go into practice, are likely before long to ease the general practitioner's task in curative medicine enormously.'[29] In the early 1960's people are still discussing how some of these hopes may yet be realized, but that is a subject that belongs to a later chapter.

But Bevan's great achievement consisted in the creation of a genuine universal, free medical service, wholly detached in its administration from the contractual apparatus of insurance (though receiving a portion of the contributions) and aiming at a standard of performance as high as the medical resources of the country were capable of achieving. 'The field in which the claims of individual commercialism come into most immediate conflict with reputable notions of social values', he wrote, 'is that of health.'[30] And he was determined that no trace of commercialism should creep in between doctor and patient in his service. He agreed later to a charge of one shilling for each prescription, but when the Labour government introduced further charges he resigned, saying that it was the 'beginning of the destruction of those social services in which Labour has taken a special pride and which were giving to Britain the moral leadership of the world'.[31]

The three pillars of the British Welfare State were the Education Act, the National Insurance Act, and the National Health Service Act. They are associated with the names of Butler, Beveridge, and Bevan—a Conservative, a Liberal, and a Socialist. When one remembers the mixed origins of social policy at the beginning of the century it is not surprising to find that the Welfare State, when it eventually saw the light, was of mixed parentage. At the time it seemed that these diverse elements were blended in a harmonious whole which expressed a single spirit and social ideal. But the harmony did not last for more than a decade, after which the various parts of the structure were subjected to criticism coming from several different directions. For the purpose of this study the two most pertinent questions are: was there really a clash of principle between Beveridge and Bevan which expressed itself in their respective creations? And was there, in spite of any such differences, a common spirit or policy, that inspired and distinguished the collection of measures that together make up the Welfare State of the post-war decade?

At first sight the principles of Beveridge and Bevan appear to stand in sharp antithesis. Beveridge offered what was strictly a minimum whereas Bevan was determined to provide an optimum. Beveridge insisted that nothing must be given by way of insurance beyond what contributions warranted, while Bevan's health service was available unconditionally. Beveridge held that assistance for which no contributions had been paid should be subject to a means test and regarded as less desirable than insurance benefits. Bevan declared that, in his case, a means test would amount to 'the creation of a two standard health service, one below and one above the salt'.[32] And that he would not have. Finally, whereas Beveridge relied for the success of his plan to a considerable extent on individual initiative and providence, it was the aim of the health service to relieve the individual of all anxiety and responsibility save that of seeking professional advice when it was needed and acting on it when it was given.

But did not these differences arise, not from any deep clash of principle between the authors of the two schemes, but from the essential differences between the two services? For Beveridge himself had demanded a national health service, of high standard, and was quite prepared that it should be offered free of charge to the patients. Nevertheless there was something about the subsistence minimum and the flat-rate contributions and benefits, fruits of Beveridge's Liberalism, which was utterly alien to the Socialism of Aneurin Bevan, and, as we shall see, they soon had no supporters. But the common element present in all the measures was the idea that social policy consisted of services rendered by the society as a whole to the society as a whole. And that idea persisted. Criticism there was in plenty, and fierce argument, but the issues at stake in the sixties turned out to be less concerned with social ideology than with social engineering.

1 R. M. Titmuss, *Problems of Social Policy*, p. 507
2 ibid., p. 504
3 A. G. B. Fisher, *Economic Progress and Social Security*, p. 23
4 Beveridge Report, para. 459
5 ibid., para. 8
6 ibid., para. 14
7 ibid., para. 31
8 *Social Insurance*, part I, 1944, Cmd. 6550, para. 1
9 H. D. Henderson, *The Inter-war Years*, pp. 192–207
10 Bulletin of the International Social Security Association, 1959, vol. XII, no. 8–9
11 Hansard (Lords), 1953, vol. 182, cols. 675–6
12 Arnold Wilson and G. S. Mackay, *Old Age Pensions*, p. 193
13 W. H. Beveridge, *Insurance for All and Everything*, pp. 6–7
14 J. L. Cohen, *Social Insurance Unified*, p. 23
15 Beveridge Report, para. 288
16 ibid., Appendix F, para. 6
17 ibid., para. 294
18 ibid., para. 369
19 *Social Insurance*, part I, paras. 12–13
20 Hansard (Lords), 1953, vol. 182, col. 677
21 Beveridge Report, para. 302
22 Hansard (Lords), 1945–6, vol. 143, col. 78
23 Henry Brackenbury, *Patient and Doctor*, pp. 149–50
24 Joan S. Clarke, in W. A. Robson (ed.), *Social Security*, pp. 92 and 121–3
25 Consultative Council on Medical and Allied Services, First Interim Report, 1920, vol. XVII, para. 3
26 Royal Commission on National Health Insurance, 1926, vol. XIV p. 138
27 ibid., p. 152
28 Harry Eckstein, *The English Health Service*, p. 142
29 A. Massey (ed.), *Modern Trends in Public Health*, p. 130
30 Aneurin Bevan, *In Place of Fear*, p. 73
31 Vincent Brome, *Aneurin Bevan*, p. 198
32 Bevan, op. cit., p. 76

PART TWO
Social policy at mid-century

*

7

Re-assessment of the Welfare State

The purpose of this short chapter is to serve as an introduction to Part Two of the book by bridging the gap between past history and the present situation, and in particular by describing the changes of mood that took place in England during the ten or twelve years following the legislation of 1946–48.

The British Welfare State was, as we have seen, the culmination of a long movement of social reform that began in the last quarter of the nineteenth century. But the final product was something that the originators of the movement had not envisaged. The forces of growth within the movement itself, combined with the influence of historic events like the great depression and the two world wars, had given this product of an evolutionary process a revolutionary character. This was how Beveridge saw it, and he was quite right. But the culmination of an evolutionary process marks the end of a past phase of history, whereas a revolution is likely to mark the beginning of a new one. Anybody surveying the scene in 1950 was bound before long to ask himself to which of these two categories the Welfare State really belonged.

There is no doubt at all that those who were preparing, during the war, the measures of which the Welfare State was to be built believed that they were laying the foundations of a new epoch in social history, and this mood persisted during the years of creative legislation after the war. Some questioning voices were raised, but they were shouted down. When, however, the period of critical appraisal began in or around 1952 the opposite view was widely expressed, namely that the Welfare State belonged to the past from which it had emerged. Future historians will probably decide that both were right, and that it contained within itself elements of both past and future and provided a necessary stepping-stone from the one to the other.

In examining the criticism levelled against the Welfare State at this time one must remember to distinguish between its two principal parts, the social security system or Beveridge plan, with its guarantee of the minimum, and the National Health Service, with its promise of the optimum. Both came under attack, but for different reasons. The social security system bore clearly upon it the marks of its origin and history. It had been constructed of measures designed to wage war against poverty, and it was in order to complete the victory over poverty, or want, and the other four giants in the path that Beveridge had elaborated his plan. When the laws that it inspired were being debated it seemed that the giants were still there; they had not vanished with the coming of peace. Times were still hard. The war had drained the country's resources, laid waste great areas in its cities, and its end was followed by a period of economic strain. The principal controls were kept in force, including the rationing of food and other consumer goods, which was not finally abolished till 1954. The nation had chosen to submit to a regime of austerity in order to prevent the reappearance in large sections of the population of the extreme poverty that had befallen them in the worst of the inter-war years. It was not unnatural to imagine that the principles on which the social security system had been built had lost nothing of their relevance in the post-war age. The methods that had been used to conquer poverty should still be appropriate for holding poverty at bay.

But this judgement underestimated the differences between the situations before and after the war, in both their economic and their social aspects. The most obvious of these was the contrast between the persistent large-scale unemployment of the 1920's and 1930's and the continuous state of full, and at times 'over-full', employment of the 1950's. This was accompanied by a rising standard of living for the bulk of the wage-earning class and a shift of interest from unemployment benefits to retirement pensions as the item in social security that mattered most. A system obsessed with the ideas of poverty and subsistence began to look out of place in a society enjoying the first-fruits of a new prosperity. But before these changes of circumstance and of mood became fully apparent, a weakness of a different kind had been revealed in the Welfare State and provoked the first wave of criticism that struck at the very roots of the system.

In February 1952 *The Times* published two articles on 'crisis in the Welfare State'. It associated the crisis, the first the new system had to face, with economic insecurity and a need for retrenchment in public expenditure.[1] It had become necessary, it said, to re-examine the principles upon which the whole system was based. About the same time two future Conservative Ministers, Iain Macleod and Enoch Powell, produced a pamphlet entitled 'The Social Services—Needs and Means'. Here too the theme was that the Welfare State had been trying to do more than it could afford, and had failed. Benefits had fallen below subsistence level, and those without other resources had to apply for additional assistance to what was in effect the old Poor Law under another name—assistance given not as a right, but at discretion and subject to a means test. This is what Beveridge himself denounced in the following year as abandonment of the 'policy of 1946'. The most economical way of abolishing want was not to distribute standard cash benefits and free services to all and sundry, whether they wanted them or not, but to concentrate scarce resources at the points where they were most needed, with the help of a test of means. 'The question therefore which poses itself,' they said, 'is not "should a means test be applied to a social service", but "why should any social service be provided without a test of need?"'[2] This came near, as Professor Titmuss asserted in his broadcast commentary, to advocating 'a new version of the nineteenth-century poor law', as far as cash benefits were concerned;[3] a return, one might say, not to the pre-Beveridge, but to the pre-Lloyd George, situation. If applied to the National Health Service (the principal target of those attacking extravagance) it would mean, as *The Times* rightly pointed out, 'a reversion from Bevanism to Fabianism',[4] for the Fabians had held that everybody should pay as much as he could afford for the public services. The scrapping of social insurance and its replacement by national assistance and a means test, though it seemed to be logically implied by the remarks of some of the critics, was hardly ever explicitly proposed, and certainly not by the authors of the pamphlet. But the idea of charging for services, including both health and education, was definitely favoured by many Conservative writers, and even more emphatically by the Liberals.

In this phase, then, the background to criticism was the urge to economize in the face of economic stringency, and the Welfare State was found to be at fault, not because it was over-obsessed with poverty, but because it did not concentrate on it enough. The typical charge was that of extravagance and the typical question 'can we afford it?' Then the mood changed. With remarkable speed the conviction spread that the time had come to give the Austerity Society decent burial and to welcome the Affluent Society in its place. And an Affluent Society should not need to maintain a complicated and expensive apparatus for waging war on poverty. To apply the Beveridge principle in 1960, said a Conservative M.P., 'is to swallow the drug after the disease has gone. For primary poverty has now almost disappeared. Full employment has lifted the mass of our working population to a level of affluence unprecedented in our social history.'[5] This estimate of the economic situation was somewhat over-optimistic, and it seemed to overlook the fact that one of the main factors in the reduction, if not abolition, of primary poverty was precisely that system of social security of which Beveridge was the chief architect. Without the 'drug' the 'disease' would have been rampant.

The proposal to which this line of thought generally led was that as much of the burden of social provision as possible should be passed over from public to private shoulders. People should be released from the system of compulsory insurance, and given the freedom to exercise personal responsibility and provide for themselves. And, when they used the public services, they should be charged according to their means. For a time little attempt was made to discover what the effects of such a transfer would be, either on the public services which would still have to function or on the private institutions which would in part replace them. The emphasis was still on the negative side, on how to get out of the false position in which the country had placed itself by carrying the legacy of the past into the present. The one thing that seemed to emerge clearly was that the critics wanted to cut down the public social services, though whether this was because the country could not afford to keep them up or because it could afford to do without them was not always obvious. What did appear certain was that, in some influential political circles, the tide was turning against the view, which had grown in strength from Lloyd George to Beveridge, that the public social services must be regarded as a permanent part of the national culture of which the people should be proud. Such statements as the following struck a different note: 'the true object of the Welfare State, for the Liberal, is to teach people how to do without it' (by a leading Liberal economist),[6] and: 'Conservatives must strive for a large reduction, in the long run, of the public social services' (by a member of the Bow group).[7]

Meanwhile events elsewhere did not seem to be moving in this direction. It is true that in France the proposal, made in 1946, to extend insurance to cover all risks and all citizens met with so much opposition that the government was forced to modify its programme,[8] while the reliance, for unemployment insurance, on private schemes and collective agreements continued unchanged. But there was no move to reduce the role of the State, and when de Gaulle tried to launch a campaign for economy, he had to bow to the protests of the champions of the public social services.[9] In the United States too, where Federal social policy always had to contend with stubborn individualists and defenders of State rights, the trend was towards a shift in the balance between statutory and voluntary services in favour of the former.[10] News was coming in of interesting developments in Sweden, in health, housing, and pensions, but probably the strongest impact was made by reports of the German legislation of 1957 which replaced a wage-related pension scheme of standard pattern by a system of universal superannuation. This term is used here to denote the familiar system of pension rights long enjoyed by civil servants and members of the armed forces, in which the pension is governed by length of service and past salary, and is normally adjusted periodically to the cost of living. The German scheme was announced with a great flourish of trumpets as a decisive step forward and away from traditional practices. Finally, when Britain began to negotiate for entry into the Common Market it was natural to compare the levels of social provision at home and in the six European Member States. Some thought that Britain might be under pressure to lower her standards if she joined. But a survey of expenditure on social security and health services published by the ILO in 1961 showed that the proportion of the national income devoted by the United Kingdom to these purposes was lower than the lowest in the Community and not quite three-fifths that of the highest.[11] The authors admitted that the figures could not be entirely reliable and must be used with caution. But, when all allowances were made, the headline in *The Times*, 'Britain lagging behind in Social Security Spending', seemed to be justified.[12]

By the end of the 1950's the emphasis in discussions of British social policy had shifted from curtailment to expansion. Much attention was being given to ways of developing more intelligent and intensive treatment of the problems of the old, the socially handicapped children, and the mentally afflicted, and legislation was under way which would increase public responsibility, and therefore public expenditure, on these subjects. In January 1962 the government announced a plan for spending five hundred million pounds in ten years (and seven hundred in all) on hospital building and development, while a rapid series of decisions resulted in the founding of seven new universities in England alone. This could hardly be called parsimonious. Finally, as the prospect of a general election drew nearer, there began to emerge from the political parties, or from semi-official groups within them, blueprints for the social services of the future bolder and more grandiose in conception than anything that had gone before.

But the approach to the subject was changing. At the time of the 1952 crisis attention had been focussed on government expenditure, and on what the Exchequer could afford. Then, when austerity gave place to affluence, it was pointed out that this was not the same as what the people could afford; a reduction of the social service budget need not lower the level of social welfare if individual families spent more on it out of their own pockets, and industrial firms continued to expand their social benefits. Finally, the sharp dichotomy between public and private expenditure yielded place to an integrated view of social provision in all its forms, for which the crucial question was what the nation could afford. The Welfare State was being transformed into the Welfare Society. The first steps in the movement of social reform, in the days of Lloyd George, had represented an assault led by political authority against the deficiencies of the economic system. Out of this had grown the idea that there was something called 'welfare' which belonged to the field of politics and depended on the action of governments, and something quite separate from it, namely income or earnings, which reflected a man's market value in the economy. The new approach fused these two elements so that together they represented the standard of living of the society, or the level and quality of its civilization, which should be set as high as the combined efforts of the polity and the economy could raise them. Antagonism had been replaced by a partnership in which the political and economic systems were pursuing the same goal, and often using the same methods.

As a result of this it was no longer a question of choosing between the three schools of thought described in Chapter 2 of this book. It was not necessary to decide whether to abolish the capitalist system, or to humanize it by social legislation, or to let it alone to solve society's problems in its own way. For events had been moving in all three directions at once. The capitalist system had been profoundly changed by central economic planning and control, by nationalization of industries, and by collective action within the economy itself. Social policy had not only done much to humanize conditions of life and work; it had altered the structure of society by admitting the working class to full membership of the community and giving its members the full status of citizenship. And the economy had, by its own efforts, not only raised the general level of prosperity but inserted so much welfare into its terms of employment that they now had little in common with the naked 'cash nexus' described by the Poor Law Commission in 1909.

All were agreed that this new situation demanded radical changes in the principles and procedures of the Welfare State as established by the legislation of 1946–8. The attacks we have already mentioned came from the Conservatives and the Liberals. The Labour Party had, in the austerity period, been the most ardent defenders of the post-war policy, and had protested against what it regarded as the betrayal of the principles of that policy by the failure to maintain benefits at the promised level. But gradually the utterances coming from the Left veered towards a frontal attack on the principles themselves. The whole apparatus, said one critic, was now obsolete. 'The system of social services we established in 1948 was designed to meet the needs of the thirties by means of administrative devices mainly invented before the First World War.'[13] The result of the extension of the social services, said another, had been that 'those who have benefited most are those who needed it least', namely the middle classes.[14] Even more significant is the fact that the Labour Party was the first to put forward, in 1957, an official scheme for a general system of superannuation to replace retirement pensions at subsistence level, which meant the abandonment of the keystone of the Beveridge plan. This elicited from Mr Macleod the comment that it was 'pleasant to see our opponents being converted to the capitalist system, and to a proposal which, in fact, intends to carry into provision for retirement the inequalities of earnings in working life'.[15] But in the first place 'inequalities of earnings', which means in this context primarily wage and salary differentials, are in principle as much a feature of a socialist as of a capitalist economy, and are found even in the 'Socialist' countries of Eastern Europe. And secondly, schemes for benefits related to earnings always operate below a fixed ceiling which excludes the grosser inequalities to which all Socialists object. The projection, in this limited way, of unequal earnings into retirement is, in fact, a natural consequence of integrating social welfare into the national culture.

Opinions may differ as to the nature of the society created by this integration. Richard Crossman referred to it at one time as 'Welfare Capitalism', and undoubtedly it is not 'capitalist' enough for some nor 'Socialist' enough for others. But in the field of social policy (always excluding education) there is a growing measure of agreement on fundamentals. It is realized that many of the old antitheses are largely imaginary—as between contributory and non-contributory social security, or between insurance and assistance; or even as between public and private services, since the latter cannot be sustained by isolated individual effort, but must be organized systems of mutual aid not unlike those operated by the State. There is little difference of opinion as to the services that must be provided, and it is generally agreed that, whoever provides them, the overall responsibility for the welfare of the citizens must remain with the State. This explains the statement made at the end of the last chapter that 'the issues at stake in the sixties turned out to be less concerned with social ideology than with social engineering'. And it is to these problems of social engineering that we must now turn.

1   *The Times*, 25 February 1952, p. 7
2   Iain Macleod and J. Enoch Powell, *The Social Services—Needs and Means*, 1952, p. 5
3   R. M. Titmuss, 'Crisis in the Social Services' in *The Listener*, 14 February 1952
4   *The Times*, 26 February 1952, p. 5
5   *Crossbow*, Autumn 1960, p. 25
6   Alan Peacock, *The Welfare Society*, p. 11
7   Geoffrey Howe, 'Reform of the Social Services' in *Principles and Practice* (Bow Group publication), p. 61

8   André Rouast et Paul Durand, *Sécurité Sociale* (2nd ed.), pp. 240–2

9   Gabriele Bremme, *Freiheit und Soziale Sicherheit*, pp. 214–20

10 V. D. Bornet, *Welfare in America*, pp. 290–5

11 ILO, *The Cost of Social Security 1949–1957*, p. 205

12 *The Times*, 24 May 1961, p. 17

13 D. V. Donnison, 'Social Services for the Family' in *The Ingleby Report—Three Critical Essays* (Fabian Society Research Series, no. 231), p. 1

14 R. M. Titmuss, *The Irresponsible Society*, p. 10

15 Conservative Political Centre, *The Future of the Welfare State*, p. 18

8

Social security

The British Welfare State, we have suggested, belonged both to the past and to the future. Those who looked at it against the background of British history were inclined to assign the Beveridge Report to the past while recognizing that the National Health Service, whether you liked it or not, marked a step into the future. But when looked at through the eyes of European observers, the picture is rather different. For they found elements both of the past and of the future in the Beveridge Report itself, and regarded the National Health Service, with its strong central control and planning powers, as not necessarily deserving of imitation by progressive societies.

In a report of the European Economic Community (the Common Market) published in 1958 the position in the six Member States was summed up as follows: 'Two different conceptions underline the systems found in the countries of the Community: some have retained the notion of social insurance, the others have directed their policy towards social security. At the level of principle, these two notions are very far apart.' But, it added, at the level of practice, the differences were not substantial.[1] The report went on to explain the contrast between the two conceptions. Insurance, it said, is built up of contracts covering specified risks, but social security is comprehensive and gives protection against all social risks. Social insurance covers only paid employees, but social security extends to all citizens. Insurance bases rights on contributions, but social security is based on 'a right directly accorded to the individual by virtue of the protection owed him by society'. Pierre Laroque, who might appropriately be described as the French Beveridge, wrote in the same sense. One of the most important features of social security, he said, was its treatment of the problem 'as one to be solved for the whole population by a general policy and under a

99

general scheme'. He also agreed about the basis of the right to benefits. In a general scheme of social security, he said, one may expect to see the 'disappearance of all connection between contributions and benefits'. It becomes 'comparatively unimportant whether the money has been obtained by means of contributions or drawn direct from public funds'.[2]

A subsequent report of the European Economic Community, dated 1962, added two further points. It distinguished between two aims, one to wage war on want, by a policy based on the concept of need, and the other to maintain incomes, for those unable to work, at a level comparable with former earnings, in which case the policy was based on the economic value of the worker. The former established a 'national minimum' by redistributing income between rich and poor; the latter adjusted the flow through time of earnings of the working population to the mutual benefit of all. Secondly, the report spoke of the sharp distinction which used to be drawn between 'classical' social insurance and 'old-style' public assistance, and maintained that the progressive obliteration of the traditional frontiers between them was 'one of the characteristic traits of the modern evolution of the system of social protection', that is to say, of the evolution from social insurance to social security. As a result, public assistance could, and must, be used as a means of filling the inevitable gaps in the coverage offered by the insurance-type services.[3]

Now it is evident that in its principles of the subsistence minimum, of rights based on contributions, and of the distinction between insurance and assistance, the Beveridge Report, on this view, belonged to the past. But by its bold introduction of universal coverage and comprehensive protection, embodied in a single scheme, it was stepping out into the future. And the European experts regarded these two principles as the really dynamic ones, in the sense that, once a universal, comprehensive scheme had been introduced, the other changes were bound to follow. On these grounds, therefore, Beveridge was, in European eyes, entitled to be hailed as the founding father of social security.

These points can best be illustrated by reference to pensions. As we have already seen, the original practice in most countries other than Britain was to relate both the contributions and the pensions to earnings. And the new type of pension described in the Common Market report is also related to earnings, but in quite a different way. Pensions of the older kind were small in amount and designed only to soften the blow of retirement. The grading of contributions, and therefore of benefits, was little more than a financial device for increasing the revenue of the pension fund and reducing the burden to be borne by taxes. With pensions of the new type the starting-point of the calculation is the idea of a decent provision for old age; and 'decent provision' is not, like subsistence, an absolute quantity, but is relative to the standard of living enjoyed by a man and his wife before retirement. It will be less than what they had then, but will not imply any catastrophic change in their manner of life. This is now generally taken to mean that the pension should equal from a half to two-thirds of a man's average earnings in the last few years of his working life, and that the proportion should be higher for those whose earnings were near the bottom of the scale. This income is, of course, expected to support both the man and his wife. Figures of this order of magnitude are found in use today, not only in countries like Germany and Sweden but also in the Soviet Union, Poland, Hungary, and Czechoslovakia, and they have been cited in proposals put forward, but not yet adopted, in Britain.[4]

The effect of such schemes, broadly speaking, is to apply to the working population in general the principle which has for a very long time governed the pensions of public servants, both civil and military. The significance of the change is expressed by saying that 'old-age pensions' are giving place to 'superannuation'. This policy cannot be given any political label, for it is found in both 'capital-ist' and 'socialist' countries. It contains in itself elements both of Socialism and of individualism, because it recognizes a universal social right in a manner that takes account of individual differences. The emphasis may be placed in one case on what society owes the worker and in another on what the worker has won for himself, and the former interpretation will favour a non-contributory scheme and the latter a contributory one. But even on this point there is no general rule. In the matter of finance pensions may be regarded as a social cost, to be borne by the whole body of tax-payers, or as a cost of production, to be borne by industry. If the second alternative is chosen, as it is even in countries as different as the USA and the USSR, it is still an open question whether in-dividual earnings should be mulcted of contributions or not. Which-ever is done, both current earnings and future pensions must be paid for out of the income of the business.

These are not characteristics of 'social insurance' as distinct from 'commercial' practices, for the same situation is found in private, or 'occupational', pension schemes. A survey conducted in 1958 revealed that about a third of these (as measured by the number of workers covered) were non-contributory. And the arguments used by experts in weighing the respective advantages of the contributory and the non-contributory systems are not concerned with any fundamental principles or with the question where the burden will ultimately fall, but rather with secondary effects of an administrative or a psychological character. A non-contributory scheme is simpler to run and easier to extend over the whole staff, and it may help to create a tie to bind the worker to the firm. But a contributory one may have the character of a joint enterprise which encourages a spirit of co-operation between employers and employed, and it may also check unreasonable demands for 'feather-bedding' and 'fringe benefits', by making it clear that such things have to be paid for.[5]

In its second report the European Economic Community, having noted the convergence of policies among its members towards the pattern we have been describing, observed that, paradoxically enough, this represented, in some of its aspects, not a departure from the 'classical' principles of insurance, but a return to them. For each beneficiary (or insured person) had, as it were, his personal account which determined the size of the pension to which he was entitled. This operated like an insurance policy, with the percentage of his earnings that was assigned to it corresponding to the insurance premium. Secondly, the system was essentially one for employees, since it was based on earnings, which meant that it was rooted in class solidarity, not in national solidarity. Consequently the European system of social security was in reality nearer to the classical model of insurance than was the Beveridge plan.[6]

This sounds plausible, but the reasoning is in fact superficial. To take the last point first, it is quite true that, in the modern pension systems, both contributions and benefits are based on earnings. But this does not mean that they are based only on wages, or even on wages and salaries. The earnings of the self-employed can be included, as in the Swedish system and in the proposal put forward by the British Labour Party. The only people to whom a scheme for maintaining income after earnings have ceased cannot possibly apply are those who do not earn, that is to say, to the rentiers. Certainly there is a difference between this approach and that of Beveridge. He wished to guarantee a national minimum to all citizens, whereas the modern pensions provide superannuation for the gainfully occupied—or they can do. And even when they are confined to employees (as is quite often the case) they are less class-based than was pre-Beveridge social insurance. For in those earlier systems there was an income limit which excluded the upper ranks of the salaried employees; they were not pensionable. But in the modern systems the income limit does not exclude a class of employees, but only a part of their incomes. They are all covered and can all get pensions, but only that portion of their earnings that falls below a specified income limit is pensionable, that is to say is used as a basis for calculating contributions, and therefore pensions. It is misleading to say that a system as comprehensive as this is rooted in class solidarity.

Then, as regards the notion of the individual account on which each pension is calculated, it is true that this is present in the modern systems and emphatically not in Beveridge. But it is wrong to think of this as the equivalent of an insurance policy. The basis of the calculation is not an account of contributions—and in fact there need not be any—but a record of employment. The pension is a part of the earnings of labour, received after retirement. The point was put very clearly in an article written by a high official to celebrate the 'Silver Anniversary' of American Social Security in 1960: 'a person's security and that of his family grow out of the work he does. He earns his future security as he earns his living, and he pays towards the cost of that security while he is earning.'[7] The right is created by work, and the contributions are an administrative instrument, which may or may not be thought to have some special merit of its own.

Modern pensions differ from classical insurance in two other important respects. First, they are protected against the effects of inflation. If 'decent provision' for old age is to make sense, it must be based on real income, not on a purely monetary calculation of the benefit corresponding to contributions paid over a long period of years. Various methods have been adopted with this end in view, some of which achieve it more accurately and completely than others. The simplest, and the commonest, is to relate the pension to average earnings in the last few years of employment, and to deal with any subsequent fall in the value of money as and when it occurs.[8] If it is desired to make the pension reflect more closely the pensioner's life history as a worker, the average may extend to his whole career, as in Germany, or to his best fifteen years, as in

Sweden, or to the last ten, as in France. The figure so obtained can then be converted into real terms by using as index the ratio of the individual's earnings to the average of all earnings at the same date. The result is not merely to compensate him for any rise in the *cost* of living, but to enable him to share in any rise in the *standard* of living, for, as the general average of earnings rise, so does the pension. The German scheme uses this method, and the Swedish uses a variant of it.[9] Where, as in Britain, there is no machinery for automatically maintaining the real value of benefits, the cash rates have to be raised from time to time, as occasion seems to demand, by *ad hoc* decisions. The increases tend to lag behind the rise in prices, and the whole matter becomes a subject of perpetual political controversy.

Secondly, it is very generally agreed that, even in a contributory scheme, there may be a transfer of income from the richer to the poorer, and not only what we described above as a readjustment of the flow of individual incomes through time. Beveridge provided for this transfer by financing pensions partly from the proceeds of progressive taxation. With flat-rate contributions there was no margin available for transfer, and in addition a transfer of contributions would violate the insurance principle by giving to the poorer a higher return on their premiums than to the richer. But with graded contributions, and the abandonment of the 'classical' principles of insurance, transfer is possible, and is generally made. Thus a scheme designed to maintain income in retirement at a proportion only of previous earnings can have built into it the amount of redistribution of income necessary to enable it also to eliminate want among those in the lowest-paid occupations.

We must now return to the British scene, and see what was happening there. It should be clear from what has been said that the new trend of policy in continental Europe involved a fairly decisive break with the principles of Beveridge. And it was only to be expected that opinion in Beveridge's own country, where his principles had but recently been incorporated in Acts of Parliament, should be reluctant to make this break. Another factor that encouraged caution in the matter of pensions was the grim vision of an ageing population which had begun to haunt men's minds. Beveridge was partly responsible for this too, since he had drawn attention to the rising cost of pensions which would result from the rising proportion of pensioners in the population. He estimated that in 1971 this proportion would reach 21% as compared with 9·6% in

1931, which was sufficiently alarming, especially to those who be-lieved that, as health improved and old people lived longer, the percentage would go on rising. The situation was changed by the rise in the birth-rate after the war, which has produced growing waves of young people to redress the balance. And in 1962, when the percentage was about 15, the Registrar General calculated that it would rise to a peak of 16·4 in the years around 1980 and then begin to fall, and that by the end of the century it would be nearly back to where it had been in the middle.[10] This altered the picture drawn by Beveridge very considerably.

The effects of these loyalties and anxieties are clearly revealed in the White Paper entitled 'Provision for Old Age' issued by the government in 1957 to explain its policy and the very modest reforms that it had decided to propose. The picture it presented was still dominated by the bogey of the ageing population. Twenty years hence, it said, 20% of the population would be pensioners and there would be (if no changes were introduced into the system) a deficit of £387 million. It would be wrong simply to pile the addi-tional cost on to the shoulders of the taxpayers, for that would mean 'drawing a blank cheque on the future'. And it would 'under-mine the protection given to the individual by the fact that the benefits he receives depend on the contributions he personally makes'. This is an astonishing statement to find in a document in which, a few pages earlier, it had been pointed out that, if a man retiring after thirty years' insurance received only the pension earned by the contributions made by himself and his employer, he would get 6s a week, whereas he was actually getting 80s. It hardly looked as if his contributions had had much to do with the preservation of his right to a decent pension.

Be that as it may, the solution was to raise contributions. But a general increase of the flat-rate payments was impossible, because 'the speed of the convoy is that of the slowest ship'; so there was to be a supplementary graduated scheme, sufficient in range to elim-inate 'the large emerging deficits'. But the extension of the State scheme in this way must not be 'excessive', for this would damage existing private, occupational pension schemes and hamper future developments in that field. The government here showed that it was loyal, not only to the Beveridge faith in contributory insurance, but also to the Beveridge principle of encouraging private saving. Not that the occupational schemes were the product of that per-sonal exercise of the virtue of thrift which Beveridge had in mind, since they were initiated and operated by the employers, but they were at least a feature of private enterprise. It was estimated that those entitled to pensions of this kind numbered in 1958 some six and a half million persons, not counting public servants. The number has risen steadily since then. The government plan did not merely refrain from competing with these schemes; it provided that the firm that ran them could contract out of the State graduated pension scheme, on behalf of themselves and their employees, provided the terms their own scheme offered were at least as good.

It is not necessary to go into the details of the plan put into effect by the Act of 1959. The flat-rate pensions continued as before and percentage contributions were levied on that part of weekly earnings lying within a 'band' from £9 to £15 (raised in 1963 to £18); as these accumulated, so the supplementary pension with which the insured worker was credited grew in a ratio determined by a mathematical formula. There was no levy on earnings below £9 because these were covered by the basic, flat-rate pension, and none on earnings above £18, because this would have involved compulsory saving on a scale that the government considered to be excessive. The system is the same as that adopted in Sweden, but the benefits obtained do not amount, as in that country, to something that can be called full superannuation. A man whose earnings fell in the middle of the 'band', and who joined the scheme at eighteen, would, according to the White Paper, have gained title only to an extra £1 a week when he retired at sixty-five. Finally, as already mentioned, firms offering alternative schemes at least as good might contract out of the graduated system, though continuing to contribute (at a slightly higher rate than those who do not contract out) to the basic, flat-rate pension scheme.

This British compromise between old-style retirement pensions and new-style superannuation has not gone down very well, and proposals for a bolder policy have come from all points of the political compass. The Labour Party had produced an official plan for superannuation before the White Paper appeared,[11] and a semi-official Liberal statement[12] and an unofficial Conservative one (by the Bow group)[13] came out in 1963. The last two were mere sketches, but all have the same broad objective of providing substantial pensions, as a proportion of past earnings, by the combined efforts of public and private enterprise. The critical point is to determine what should be the respective roles of these two sectors of the social system. Should they be complementary or alternatives?

It is safe to say that if the private sector has any role at all (and in Communist countries, of course, it has none) it must be, up to a point, complementary. For no modern government could fail to guarantee at least a sufficient minimum to everybody. Above that the field can be left wholly free to private enterprise, which is the line along which the Liberals seem to be thinking, or it may be occupied mainly by a public scheme, with a possibility of contracting out so strictly limited as to have little effect, as in Sweden. Or the two sectors may be given, in principle, equal status as alternatives, as in the British plan of 1959.

The choice of policy will depend very much on one's conception of the responsibility of the State, on the possibility of guaranteeing the continuing solvency of private schemes, and on the effectiveness of measures to ensure that a man can take his full pension rights in a private scheme with him when he changes his job. It will also depend on whether one believes that the pensions men get when they retire should vary according to the fortunes of the industry, or even the individual firm, in which they have been employed during their working lives. Should occupational pension schemes be competitive among themselves, and therefore a means for attracting labour from one industry or business to another? It is interesting to note that in Sweden contracting-out was allowed (apart from the case of the self-employed) only on the basis of a collective agreement between a trade union and an employers' organization. But, if all private schemes were formed in this way, and always subject to government approval, the difference between this and a general public system would be reduced to small proportions.

We have been talking about pensions without explaining what they are. In most cases a pension is an income to which a person becomes entitled on passing a 'point of no return' and which is payable till death. The pensioner has, for example, finally retired from a particular employment or from all employment, has reached a certain age, or has permanently lost the health and strength necessary for earning his living. But there are some other kinds of pensionable status which, though due to events that are strictly speaking irreversible, are not treated as permanent, such as that of the widow, and sometimes of the deserted wife, who may marry again, or of the orphan who will in due course become independent. A status is not an objective fact, but is created by the political decision that defines it. Old age may begin at sixty, or sixty-five or seventy, and the criterion may be the same for men and women, or different.

British policy has stuck to sixty for women and sixty-five for men, although these figures are now rather on the low side and there is no obvious reason why men and women should not be treated alike, especially when the needs of both husband and wife are covered by a single superannuation income. But in the British system these are only the minimum qualifying ages; following Beveridge's recommendation, the pension is not payable until the pensioner has retired. The advantages of this are obvious. The pension is not paid until it is needed, the national bill is reduced, and there is an incentive for old people to go on working, because for every year that they do so they earn a small addition to their ultimate pension. The disadvantage is that 'retirement' must be defined, and there is no effective way of doing this except by the 'earnings rule'. The principle is that when you retire your earnings cease but, as a concession, you may earn up to a fixed maximum without loss of pension rights; after that progressive deductions are made from the pension until the point is reached at which it disappears. Pensioners are inclined, instead of being grateful for the concession, to be indignant at the deductions, perhaps because the declaration of income from work that the pensioner must make is reminiscent of the 'means test'. At seventy a man's pension becomes unconditional, and the view is now strongly held in some quarters that the 'earnings rule' should be dropped altogether. This would mean that the 'retirement pension' would once more become an 'old-age pension', as it is in most countries.

The same issue, in a more acute form, has arisen in the case of widows. A widow receives, under the British system, an 'allowance' for herself and her children, at a rate more generous than those used in other cases, for a period of thirteen weeks after the death of her husband. This is intended to give her time to arrange her affairs. She then receives a 'widowed mother's allowance' at a slightly lower rate as long as she has dependent children. Thereafter, if she has reached the age of fifty, she gets a pension at the standard rate. But this is in effect a retirement pension given in advance of the normal age because it is not thought reasonable to assume that a woman of fifty will be able to find a job by which to earn her living. It is therefore subject to the 'earnings rule'. The idea is that there is no logical reason why a woman of fifty who is earning her living should get a pension simply because she once had a husband, whereas a single woman in the same position does not. But to insist that a woman who has been a housewife and mother for twenty years or more must find herself a job by which she can earn her living may obviously cause very real hardship in many cases. The 'widowed mother's allowance' is also subject to the 'earnings rule', and this is even less easy to justify. For, as recent studies have shown, the situation of a 'fatherless family' cannot be fairly assessed by comparing income with the cost of living.[14] The difficulties faced by the mother are formidable, and there is a strong feeling that she should have the full benefit of anything she can earn by her own efforts, in addition to the allowance, as long as her children are dependent. The argument that this would encourage her to go out to work, when she ought to stay at home and look after the children, would have force only if the allowance were amply sufficient to meet her reasonable demands, which it is not. In January 1964 a Bill making some minor improvements was introduced, but the Minister refused to consider abolishing the 'earnings rule' either for widows or for pensions in general, partly on the grounds of expense, and partly because it would mean putting the clock back twenty years to the idea of unconditional old-age pensions.[15]

This does not reveal a very clear understanding of the situation. All countries give 'unconditional' pensions at a certain age—at seventy (for men) in Britain and Canada, sixty-seven in Sweden, sixty-five in Germany, and so on. All countries recognize that the need may arise earlier, and there must be some kind of a 'buffer state' to ease the transition from full self-support to full pensioner status. This takes various forms. In Britain there is the conditional retirement pension at sixty-five, and in Canada a system of statutory ('categorical') old-age assistance from the same age.[16] Or particular causes of incapacity to earn may be treated as a kind of premature old age. This is, as we have just seen, the case with widows of fifty, and a similar concession is made in Germany to men of sixty who have been unemployed for a full year.[17] Very commonly injury or poor health, which reduces or terminates the capacity to earn, is treated in the same way. And here, since the pension is definitely a substitute for earnings, it is adjusted to the extent of the incapacity; the full pension is paid for complete inability to work, and an appropriate fraction of the pension for partial incapacity. This is the category of 'disability' or 'invalidity' which we find in most systems. Thus we may say that, in general, pensions, which are allowances paid when circumstances indicate that the capacity to earn appears to have finally come to an end, are assimilated to a common model, that applied to old age and retirement. At one time suggestions were made that the reverse process should be adopted, and that old-age pensions should be assimilated to disability pensions, and be given only on a doctor's certificate that the man (or woman) was no longer capable of working. But this idea, fortunately, seems to have been dropped.[18]

The coverage of short-term loss of earnings through sickness and unemployment raises different questions. As long as it remains short-term, the application of the general principles of social security (with wage-related contributions and benefits) presents no difficulty, assuming that it is thought necessary to apply it. But only thirty of the 102 countries covered by the United States survey in 1961 had found it necessary in the case of unemployment. The others relied on private, including trade union, benefit systems, or on public assistance—possibly of the special 'categorical' variety. This has always been the case in France, but in 1958 a massive collective agreement was concluded between employers and unions for unemployment insurance, which covers a very large proportion of industrial workers and is obligatory on all firms belonging to the industries that are party to it.[19] The main problem to be faced in unemployment insurance is not the purely fiscal one—unless unemployment assumes 'mass' proportions and endures. It arises from the fear that benefits adequate to maintain the unemployed family at a decent standard of living will impede the mobility of labour. There may be, as Professor Allan Fisher put it, a clash between progress and security, for economic progress may depend on flexibility in the labour market. In theory benefit is payable only to those genuinely unable to find a suitable job, but it is impossible to enforce this rule when the only 'suitable' jobs are a long way off in a town in which there is, perhaps, an acute housing shortage, whereas the unemployed family has a decent home and a couple of children doing well in the local school. It is easier to live on the benefit than to migrate, if the benefit is sufficiently generous. The solution is to fix the benefit appreciably below average earnings and to adopt all possible positive means to ease the impact of 'redundancy' and to help those thrown out of work to overcome the obstacles that separate them from the jobs in which they are really wanted.

Much is being done on these lines both by the government and by industry itself. The effects of temporary fluctuations can be mitigated by limiting recruitment, work-sharing, and absorbing the redundant workers in other departments or in another branch of the same firm. When the change in demand for labour is of a more permanent character, something can be done to phase redundancy, to give long notice to those who must leave, to pay them compensation, and to help them to get new jobs, both by providing training and by contributing to the cost of a move to another district.[20] The Ministry of Labour runs training centres for disabled servicemen and for the unemployed in need of special help. And in 1960 it dispensed some 2,500 lodging allowances and a number of travel warrants to help men to migrate to new areas.

Cash benefits during short-term sickness have lost something of their importance owing to the large number of employees who now get sick pay from their employers. But, as a recent survey showed, the proportion ranges from 88% of those in professional and salaried posts to only 41% of unskilled workers, and the amount and duration of the benefits vary greatly.[21] So it would not be possible to confine State insurance to the longer illnesses and to 'invalidity' (or permanent incapacity) unless steps were first taken to generalize and standardize the private schemes.

We come finally to National Assistance. The situation deplored by Beveridge has continued, and National Assistance is regularly and extensively used to supplement insurance benefits. In 1962 72% of the weekly allowances were of this kind. Looking at it from the opposite angle, 28% of the pensioners and 16·5% of the widows were drawing assistance allowances in addition to their pensions. This may seem surprising, since both the benefits and the allowances are in theory fixed at or around subsistence level, whatever that may mean. The basic pension for a married couple has been running at about one-third of the average earnings of a manual worker in industry, which is low by European standards, and at about one-fifth for a single person. This is not subsistence. The basic National Assistance rate has generally been the same or slightly less. But it does not cover rent, for which an additional sum is given, and the allowance can be further increased at discretion to meet other needs, and that is why it can exceed, and so supplement, insurance benefits. The National Assistance Board does, in fact, make some use of a 'needs test' as well as of a 'means test'.

These facts seem to support the view that, in so far as primary poverty still exists in the Affluent Society, it is a reproach, not to the affluent economy, but to the niggardly social services. But this is no more than a half-truth. An enquiry conducted by Mrs Cole

Wedderburn showed that well over half the pensioners had little or
nothing in the way of personal income; they had not been able to
make any provision for old age, but then, of course, their working
life had not been spent in an affluent society. So it can be argued
that, if they are now living in abject poverty, it is because the State
has failed in its duty towards them. But subsequent analysis of the
Ministry of Labour's survey of current expenditure in families of
all kinds showed that, while it is true that nearly all the families
nearest to the poverty line lack an earning member, and are therefore abnormal, in the next layer with incomes not more than 5%
higher, families living mainly on earnings were 'almost as numerous'
as the former abnormal type, and as you go up the scale, the proportion rises.[22] And one must ascend the income ladder for quite a
long way before personal saving on a significant scale becomes a
possibility, let alone a probability. The population is not sharply
divided into affluent workers on the one hand and impoverished
pensioners on the other.

One may conclude that, if insurance benefits are insufficient of
themselves to support a family, the need for supplementary allowances in many cases will continue, even in an Affluent Society. And
the only way finally to remove the invidious distinction between the
two parts of the income derived from public funds (the so-called
insurance and assistance components) is to amalgamate them
administratively into a single payment, and to get rid of the out-of-
date conception of 'subsistence', which implies that there is some
objective method of determining at any given moment what are
the necessities of life. A step in this direction was taken, at least
verbally, when in 1959 the government declared that it had come to
the conclusion that 'the time has come when it is right to move to
a higher standard' and so to give to those in receipt of assistance
'a share in increasing national prosperity'.[23] If those last words
were taken literally, the distinction between insurance and assistance
would be undermined. For assistance would then be only another way
of injecting into the insurance scheme from outside (i.e. from tax
revenue) that element of redistribution of income which, as we
have seen, is incorporated into the graduated superannuation-type
systems of the Continent. These, by providing benefits that are
adequate even for the lowest income groups, reduce the category
of cases requiring additional help to those that really are anomalies.
And in these there is nearly always some factor present in addition
to the purely financial one. When this is so, it is appropriate to

treat cash benefits as an item in a service concerned with general social welfare, which is the subject of the next chapter.

1 *Exposé sur la situation sociale dans la Communauté*, 1958, p. 71

2 *International Labour Review*, vol. LVII, p. 566; J. E. Russell (ed.), *National Policies for Education, Health and Social Services*, pp. 275–6

3 European Economic Community, *Études—Série Politique Sociale. Sécurité Sociale*, 1962, pp. 14–23

4 US Department of Health, Education and Welfare, *Social Security Programs throughout the World*, 1961; Labour Party, *National Superannuation*, 1957

5 G. A. Hosking, *Pension Schemes and Retirement Benefits*, pp. 56–8; M. Pilch and V. Wood, *Pension Schemes*, pp. 56–9

6 EEC, *Sécurité Sociale*, p. 8

7 *OASIS*, August 1960, p. 8

8 US Department of Health etc., op. cit., p. xiii

9 *Industry and Labour*, 1957, no. 6, pp. 11–13; Ernst Michanek, *Sweden's new National Pension Insurance;* Paul Caesar, *Sozialversicherung*, p. 91

10 Registrar General, Fourth Quarterly Return, 1962, Appendix E

11 Labour Party, *National Superannuation*

12 M. P. Fogarty, *Security in a New Society*

13 Bow Group, *Old People in Britain*

14 Margaret Wynn, *Fatherless Families*, p.16

15 Hansard (Commons), 1964, vol. 687, col. 1095

16 J. H. Richardson, *Economic and Financial Aspects of Social Security*, pp. 116–17

17 Caesar, op. cit., p. 98

18 B. Abel-Smith, *The Reform of Social Security*, p. 30

19 *Industry and Labour*, 1959, vol. XXI, pp. 263–6

20 M. P. Fogarty in J. L. Meij (ed.), *Internal Wage Structure*, pp. 80–1

21 *The Times*, 23 January 1964

22 Dorothy Cole, *The Economic Circumstances of Old People*, pp. 100–1; D. Cole Wedderburn, *Sociological Review*, vol. X, no. 3, pp. 275–6

23 Quoted in Tony Lynes, *National Assistance and National Prosperity*, p. 16

9

Social welfare

Opinions may differ as to the full and perfect definition of social welfare, but there is general agreement about its central core. It refers to a service that is personal, and of a general rather than a specialized kind; its aim is to help someone to make the best of life in face of the disabilities with which he is afflicted, or the difficulties which confront him, and have either already defeated him or threaten to do so. It offers support to the weak and aims either at rehabilitation or at adjustment to circumstances that cannot be changed. The highest achievement to which it can aspire is well described in a sentence taken from a circular of the Ministry of Health about the welfare of the disabled. The welfare services, it says, should aim at ensuring that 'all handicapped persons, whatever their disability, shall have the maximum opportunity of sharing in and contributing to the life of the community, so that their capabilities are realized to the full, their self-confidence developed, and their social contacts strengthened'.[1]

In a book about London government in the 1960's the welfare services are defined as those 'provided by local authorities to give assistance, other than medical and financial, to those needing such assistance through handicaps of age, or physical, mental or social infirmity'. And the catalogue of the people receiving this kind of assistance includes the old, blind, deaf, dumb, permanently disabled or mentally handicapped, the children deprived of a home life, the unmarried mothers, the homeless, problem families, and the 'down and outs'.[2] The first thing to notice is that the welfare services are described as 'local', and this is generally accepted as proper. They are regarded as the concern of the neighbourhood, as services rendered by people who know the district and are acquainted with the circumstances of the applicants. Secondly we note that medical care is excluded because it is highly specialized, and financial aid because it is not a personal service. But it must be remembered that financial aid may fail to achieve its purpose unless accompanied by some personal help and advice on how to use it. Similarly medical treatment must often be accompanied or followed by welfare service, as in the case of a crippled child or a mother of a family who has to undergo an operation. There is also welfare work to be done in schools, on housing estates, in youth clubs and among discharged prisoners, and in other groups of persons which have not been included in the London list because the welfare work is undertaken by the specialized authority concerned. We come, in fact, to the conclusion that what we are seeking to define is not so much a service, or a group of services, as an element that is present in many services. And one of the most difficult problems with which the policymaker is faced is to discover how to distribute functions and responsibilities in such a way that both the general welfare element and the various specialized elements are properly cared for, and so integrated in the treatment of each case that the person served is not torn to pieces by those who are desperately trying to help him.

Finally we notice that the London list falls into two parts, the physically and mentally handicapped, and those suffering from a 'social infirmity'. The first of these categories is fairly clear cut; the second is not. It may seem that the 'deprived child', the homeless, and the problem family obviously belong in it, but what about the unhappy marriage that has not led to separation, or the over-burdened mother whose family has not yet become a 'problem', or still more the young couple who want advice on how to plan their family in advance so as to avoid that particular 'social infirmity'? Obviously marriage guidance and family planning are services in which the welfare element is very strong indeed, but the crucial question is whether the State should engage in them, or leave them to voluntary organizations, or perhaps actively discourage them. And here, on the fringe, as it were, of the area of public welfare, we no longer find general consensus, but observe that policy differs from country to country. In one country marriage guidance may be subsidized from public funds, and practised to some extent officially in matrimonial courts, while family planning is frowned on or left severely alone. In another, such as India, family planning occupies a prominent place in government policy, but marriage guidance, other than by the families concerned, is quite alien to the national culture.

Such, then, are the scope and some of the problems of modern

welfare policy. The use of the adjective 'modern' is justified because
the welfare services, as we know them, took shape only in comparatively recent times, following on the whittling down and final
transformation of the Poor Law and Public Assistance which took
place nearly everywhere during this century, and particularly in the
inter-war period. It has been said of Britain that 'the welfare services
department is as it were the residuary legatee of the old public
assistance department'.[3] The word 'residuary' is appropriate, because the heritage consisted of those bits and pieces of a welfare
service which could not be assigned to specialized agencies when
the Poor Law was broken up. And even these bits and pieces were
not handed over as going concerns; the charge given to the welfare
authorities was to create services of a new kind, partly to replace
those which were marked with the stamp of pauperism, and partly
to supplement them.

The break with the past was, as we have seen, more complete than
in many European countries, where the trend was towards developing the welfare element within the 'social assistance' service.
There had been signs, both in America and in Britain, of the urge
to advance along these lines. As far back as 1929 New York re-
named its Poor Law 'Public Welfare Law', and gave it the task of
doing everything necessary for those unable to maintain themselves,
in order to 'restore such persons to a condition of self-support',
and also to help those 'liable to become destitute' to escape this
fate.[4] But this was not the pattern that was destined to prevail.
Similarly in the late 1930's the London County Council proposed to
re-christen its Public Assistance Committee 'Social Welfare Committee' and to call its relieving Officers 'Welfare Officers'.[5] But here
too events took a different path. When the new name was introduced
it was given, not to the old committee and officers, but to new ones.
The significance of this step was strongly underlined by Aneurin
Bevan when he introduced the National Assistance Bill. He was
speaking about the care of the aged. 'We have decided,' he said,
'to make a great departure in the treatment of old people. The
workhouse is to go. Although many people have tried to humanize
it, it was in many respects a very evil institution. We have determined that the right way to approach the problem is to give the
Welfare Authorities, as we shall now describe them, the power to
establish separate Homes.'[6]

But the price that welfare had to pay for the right to extend
the circle of its customers was acceptance of a limitation of its

powers. The task of Public Assistance in the 1930's was 'to provide such relief as may be necessary for the lame, impotent, old, blind, and such other persons as are poor and unable to work'.[7] Guardians in charge of paupers, and only of paupers, could safely be given this wide discretion in the discharge of their duties. But the new welfare authorities, whose clientele was not limited in this way, were obliged to start, so to speak, from scratch, and were allowed to do only what was explicitly authorized by statute. The authorizations came gradually, leaving gaps to be filled as they were revealed by experience. The National Assistance Act (Part III), for instance, imposed on local authorities the duty of providing residential accommodation for the aged and infirm, but gave no power to do anything more for them. And the only way, until 1962, in which a local Council could see that infirm old people got domestic help and some recreational facilities was by subsidizing a voluntary society that would provide them, unless it could obtain the sanction of a Private Act of Parliament.[8] It is true that the Act gave wider and vaguer powers (not duties) for 'promoting the welfare' of other permanently handicapped persons, but these could only be exercised in accordance with a scheme approved by the Minister. The power was converted into a duty by Ministerial order in the case of the blind immediately after the Act was passed, but in the case of other disabilities not until 1960.[9]

These limitations and delays caused much exasperation among those responsible for welfare, and have provoked much criticism from students of social policy. But it should be realized that the policy-makers were facing a new situation, and that in such circumstances those who draft the statutes are liable to err on the side of caution. When, in 1940, the Unemployment Assistance Board dropped the word 'unemployment' from its title and undertook to distribute supplementary pensions to impoverished old people outside the ambit of the Poor Law, it was instructed to carry out its task 'in such manner as may best promote the welfare of pensioners', and it took its welfare duties very seriously.[10] But it found things rather more difficult than it had expected, for, as it said in its Report for 1944, 'in undertaking a national service with welfare responsibility for old people in need of financial assistance the Board was breaking new ground'. Although much had been done by voluntary organizations and something by 'the more progressive Public Assistance Authorities', there was as yet 'no common body of doctrine or practice' with regard to social welfare.[11]

This statement may sound surprising, considering its date, but it was true. The problems of social welfare were novel ones, and a clue to the nature of their novelty can be found in the title of a paper submitted twenty-five years earlier to a conference of American social workers; it was called 'Casework above the Poverty Line'.[12] When a welfare service is offered to persons below the poverty line, and to them only, its purpose clearly is to lift them up to, and just safely above, the line. But when they are already above the poverty line there is no easily recognizable ceiling to work to, and it may not even be clear to whom the service should be offered. Again, the situation of those below the line is so desperate that, even if the status of pauper is not precisely defined in law, it will probably be assumed that they should gratefully accept what is given, in the form and place in which it is offered (even if that place be the workhouse), and should not claim the right to pick and choose or make conditions. And, if the service is of the old Poor Law type, or regarded as such, it cannot go out to look for those who need its help, because they would be tainted by its touch. It must wait for them to come to it unless, by committing an offence or becoming a public nuisance, they have forfeited their right to be treated as free agents. It was realized that these principles could not be applied to people who, like the Assistance Boards' pensioners, were not paupers, and still less to those whose trouble was not due primarily to poverty. The new welfare services must decide how far they should go in publicizing their wares, and we may note that the giving of information about the available services was the first of the activities assigned by the National Assistance Act to the local welfare authority. They must also know what standard of welfare to aim at—whether a tolerable minimum or the best that can be hoped for in an imperfect world. And they must take account of two possible objections to an indefinite expansion of their services—the expense falling on public funds, and the fear that they may trespass too freely on the privacy of the citizen and use undue pressure to persuade, or even to compel, people to accept what they, the experts, believe will be good for them.

The best way to see how these and other similar questions have arisen and been answered is to take a look at the most important types of welfare service that are generally being operated today. We will begin with the children. The right of a public authority to enter the home in the interests of the child had long been recognized in the case of education and of infant health; recognition came more slowly when the question was one of the vaguer notion of welfare. The approach lay through action to punish cruelty. The story can be traced back to the Select Committee of 1871 on 'the best means of preventing the destruction of the lives of infants put out to nurse for hire by their parents', and through a series of not very effective measures to deal with deliberate crime and gross neglect, down to the Children's Act of 1933, which took the crucial step across the gap that lies between the punishment of crime and the promotion of welfare. This Act contained, in addition to a formidable array of penal clauses, a section providing that children 'in need of care and protection' could be brought before a Juvenile Court (without being charged with an offence) and placed in care of a 'fit person', who might be, and generally was, the local authority. Thus judicial procedure could be used, not only to punish parents for cruelty, but also to take their children away if they could not be trusted to look after them properly.

In 1946 there were 13,000 children (in England and Wales) 'in care' under this law, in addition to over 32,000 necessitous children maintained by the Public Assistance authorities.[13] But there was evidence to show that the new welfare approach had not fully prevailed over the old penal one. A voluntary committee under Mrs Hubback, which investigated the situation at that time, reported that in practice it proved difficult to do anything for the child until steps had been taken to prosecute the offending parent or guardian, and this was possible only if it could be shown that the neglect or ill-treatment of the child was 'wilful'. This was equally true of the work of the National Society for the Prevention of Cruelty to Children (which was authorized to co-operate with the authorities), whose officers (known as the 'cruelty men') operated by prosecuting or threatening to prosecute. And, as the Committee observed, 'it is difficult to be both a prosecutor and a social worker'.[14]

Meanwhile the Curtis Committee had been given the task of enquiring how best to provide for 'children deprived of normal home life with their own parents and relatives'. It had interpreted its assignment as being confined to the study of the various ways of disposing of them after they had been removed from their own homes. In its recommendations as to treatment the Report (1946) followed the line of thought generally current at the time, namely that children taken from their homes should be put to live in conditions as much like a home as possible. Adoption and 'boarding-out' were probably the best solutions, provided the host families were well chosen. The Committee summed up its thoughts on this difficult issue by saying that, although there might be a greater risk of 'acute unhappiness' in a foster home, 'a happy foster home is happier than life as generally lived in a large community'.[15] This was no doubt true of the typical 'community' as it existed then, namely a big barrack-type institution, but the Committee looked with some favour on the intermediate solution of putting the children in smaller Homes or groups of cottages where more of the atmosphere of family life could be created.

One of the most important recommendations made by the Committee concerned administration. They insisted that the whole responsibility for children 'in care' should be entrusted to a single committee of the local authority, with a Children's Officer of senior rank as its executive agent. Opinions differed, they said, as to which committee should assume the responsibility, but 'the one point of agreement is that it should not be the Public Assistance Committee or be capable of being described as the Public Assistance Committee under another name'.[16] This recommendation, which was accepted, marks one of the last stages in the 'break-up' of the Poor Law before its final liquidation. And it was a 'break-up' in a form of which the Webbs would have approved. For although the Children's Department was to have the whole responsibility for the welfare of the children, it was not to be, like the old Poor Law, a general purpose authority. For the specialized services in education, health and the rest the 'deprived child' would use the same agencies as all other children. But the Curtis Committee, unlike the Minority Report, realized that, when this specialization had been carried as far as it would go, welfare would still remain as something that needed to have a service of its own, and a very important one.

Legislation and Ministerial orders gave effect to the main recommendations of the Curtis Committee, and in some crucial respects went beyond them. The Committee had not proposed any way, other than by an order of the court, by which children could be taken into care who were not destitute, deserted, or orphaned, but whose homes nevertheless failed miserably to meet their needs. And it had said nothing about welfare work in the children's own homes, because it considered that this fell outside its terms of reference. It had, in fact, not completed in its mind the transition from the judicial to the welfare approach, and it did not fully face the difficult question of deciding how far it was legitimate to invade the rights of the parent in the interest of the welfare of the child. But subsequent legislation dealt with these matters.

By the Acts of 1948 and 1952 the local authority was given, not only the power, but the duty to enquire into any case that came to its notice where there might be a child 'in need of care and protection'. If it found such a state of affairs, it must take the child into its care, subject to the consent of the parents or guardian. Experience has shown that in the majority of cases this is readily forthcoming, and in fact very often it is the parents who take the initiative and ask for help. In cases of desertion, or where the parents are hopelessly unreliable or obstructive, the local authority can 'assume parental rights', subject to confirmation by the court if there is an appeal. Then the consent of the parents is no longer necessary, and the child cannot be withdrawn from care at will. In addition to this it was laid down that, in deciding what to do with the child, the highest priority of all must be given to keeping it in its own home; and if it was thought necessary to remove it, every effort must be made to improve conditions in the home so that the child could be taken back as soon as possible.

By these measures it was clearly established that the first consideration must be for the welfare of the child, but that the rights of the parents must not be overruled unless this was absolutely necessary. But it was soon pointed out that the recognition that the proper place for a child was with its own family, in its own home, had further implications. It was not enough to prepare the home to receive the child back from care; steps should be taken to prevent the home from ever getting into a state that made it necessary to take the child away. Had not the Hubback Committee called for a general welfare service of family case-workers to help families which were getting into difficulties?[17] In reply to these protestations the three Ministries concerned issued a Joint Circular in 1950 which expressed full approval of the action proposed and said that the powers to undertake it already existed. All that was needed was to co-ordinate the exercise of these powers by setting up joint committees, which should include representatives of appropriate voluntary organizations. Then in 1963 came an Act which opened the door wide by authorizing local authorities to give 'advice, guidance and assistance' with a view to 'diminishing the need to receive children into or keep them in care'. One might have imagined that these powers already existed. For what, otherwise, was the point of the Children's Department of the Home Office saying in its Report for 1961 that 'long and intensive case-work may be necessary to enable a family to keep together and maintain a reasonable mode of living'?[18] The truth is that even those directly engaged in the work were not very sure what their powers were, and often did not want to know. Any energetic local committee was pretty certain that it was exceeding its statutory authority, and realized that nothing was likely to be done about it, provided it was careful not to enter any expenditure in a form which could not be passed by the auditor.

The development of policy along these lines has been accompanied by a change of ideas about what to do with children who have been removed from their homes and taken into care. One of the strongest impressions left by the Curtis Committee's Report was that large institutions are quite unsuitable for young children. Opinion veered in the direction of believing that what children really needed was a 'substitute home', where they could be looked after by a 'house mother' or a 'foster mother'. And for a time action was guided largely by this belief. But the notion of a 'substitute home' only makes sense if there has been a complete and final break with the real home, and the policy of the 1950's, and still more of the 1960's, has been directed towards preventing any such break from being made if it can possibly be avoided. The pattern of action includes co-operation with the parents before the child is taken into care (to prevent this if possible), while it is in care (to prepare the home for its return), and after it comes back (to help it to settle down). So the 'substitute home' is an appropriate solution only when the natural home fails to respond to this treatment, and more use is being made of Homes of the larger type, which are regarded as a sort of boarding-school where the children can be visited and from which they can go home from time to time during the holidays. Thus the child is not subjected to the strain of having to reconcile two conflicting family loyalties. And it should be remembered that in many cases the local authority is being asked by the parents to do what is often done by neighbours and relatives, to look after the child during an emergency (such as illness) which may be of relatively short duration. This happens more frequently now than it used to do, partly because so many women friends and relations are working, and therefore not free to help, and partly because of the diminishing reluctance to invoke the assistance of a public service.

Turning now to the welfare services for old people, we find that

the story resembles in many respects that of the care of children.
There is the same original inadequacy of the powers assigned to the
local authorities, and their belated increase. And there is the same
legacy of Poor Law institutions, and the determination to eliminate
them as fast as possible. These barrack-like ex-workhouses have, in
the minds of old people, an almost penal character. Professor
Townsend, who has made the most intensive study of Homes for
the aged, tells how a matron in one of the modern Homes said:
'It's the one threat of discipline we have here—to send them back to
the old institution.'[19] This is an impossible situation. After the war
the authorities made a considerable effort to build smaller Homes
in which some consideration could be given to the special needs of
the old. Much can be done by suitable architectural design and
furnishing to make the inmates comfortable and help the crippled
or rheumatic to get about and look after themselves with the minimum of help from others. It does not need much imagination to
realize that it must be made easy for old people to get suitable
spectacles and hearing-aids, that they need, not only to be regularly
seen by a doctor, but to have the services of a chiropodist (very
important) and perhaps a physiotherapist, and that there should be
somebody handy who is a qualified nurse.

All this is well understood, but the translation of these ideas into
practice is inevitably a slow business. This is partly due to the
sheer magnitude of the task. In spite of the progress made since the
war, 37,000 old people were still living in former Poor Law Institutions in 1960, and there were very nearly another 37,000 in other
types of public authority Homes.[20] The sympathetic management
of life in the Homes depends on having enough staff, sufficiently
intelligent, and willing to stay long enough to understand the problems with which they are supposed to deal. With the employment
opportunities now open to women it is difficult to get staff of any
kind, and the turnover rate is high. Finally, many of the unhappi-
nesses that come with old age can never be overcome, and none of
them without the active co-operation of the old people themselves.
And the physical environment, however well designed, cannot of
itself elicit this. One of the most depressing features of Professor
Townsend's study is the picture it draws of old people sharing a
house and meeting one another every day without developing any
real system of communication between them or any intimate
social relationships.[21]

So policy came to be directed more and more towards trying to

keep old people at home, where they could live a normal community life. As the Director General of the Norwegian Health
Service observed in 1957: 'The most common solution is to build
old people's homes. In Norway, however, the emphasis has gradually been placed on allowing as many of the elderly as possible to
continue living outside special institutions, in ordinary residences
but preferably adapted to their needs.'[22] British policy has fallen
into line with this trend, and all housing programmes include
dwellings, usually bungalows or rows of two-storey houses, specially
designed for old people. The old idea, firmly fixed in some people's
minds, that old people must live on the ground floor, is gradually
losing force, and this had made it possible to accommodate the
aged in apartment blocks. Sometimes a section of a block of flats
is devoted to the elderly, being specially equipped for this purpose
and provided with the services that old people need. The use made
of a multi-storey block of flats at Wythenshawe, furnished with
lifts and access balconies, has, we are told, 'shown that old people
can feel more secure high above the street, and can prefer to be
away from the noise, particularly when they are within sight and
easy reach of a shopping centre'.[23] And they can live a companion-
able life with their neighbours, which is perhaps the most important
thing of all.

But it is not only the 'residences' that have to be adapted; the
same is true of the whole social environment. Every recent enquiry
has shown how many old people, or elderly couples, apparently
living alone, are in fact being looked after by a daughter or a
daughter-in-law without whose care they would have had to go
into a Home. This shows what can be done, if the necessary service
is provided. But other enquiries have shown that there are limits to
what can be undertaken by members of the family. In one place it
was found that one in thirteen of the old people visited 'were
causing great strain on the younger generation' and turning somebody into a drudge.[24] In another a daughter wrote to apply for a
place in a Home for her mother, because her husband had threatened
to leave her, taking the children with him, if she continued to neglect them in order to look after her mother.[25] So, if old people are
really to be absorbed into the community, there must be a considerable expansion of the public and voluntary social services available
to them. This is what is envisaged under the title of 'community
care', a subject to which we will return later, both in this chapter
and in the next.

The third main category of persons for whom welfare services must provide is that of the handicapped—the blind, deaf, dumb, crippled, and mentally sub-normal. In their case the expansion of the services offered is due at least as much to the increase in our understanding of the nature of their disabilities and the improvement in the techniques of treatment as to the greater sense of responsibility towards the unfortunate. The effect has been to shift the emphasis from taking care of the helpless to overcoming their helplessness by education and training for a special kind of life, which may be tolerable and acceptable, though inevitably limited in scope. This began more than a hundred years ago for the blind when Valentin Haüy invented and Braille perfected an embossed script that could be read with the fingers, and it has continued with the evolution of methods of training the blind to pursue a variety of occupations in which they can become at least as proficient as those with normal sight, and sometimes more so. Similarly ways were found to enable the deaf and the dumb to communicate, and even to break the isolation of those born deaf, who have never heard the sound of words. In all this much has been done, not only by charitable societies, but also by the associations of the blind and the deaf themselves.

There was a time when it was widely believed that spastics were mentally deficient and mongols ineducable, but the falsity of these beliefs has been exposed, and methods of treatment have been developed which allow these afflicted people to enjoy the fullest life that their disability permits. All these services have the element of welfare in them, because they involve personal devotion to the interests and care of the patient. But, of course, there have been advances also in the strictly medical and surgical techniques which may ameliorate or even cure the disability, and this is most markedly so in the case of those crippled by accident or illness. Consequently the borderline between medical treatment and welfare becomes blurred, and many services containing a welfare element may be entrusted to the health authorities, and become to this extent specialized. The education and employment authorities are interested as well. In England, for instance, special schools for the blind are run by the education authorities, but home teachers for the blind, and the provision of leisure occupations, come under welfare. An Act of 1944 authorized the Ministry of Labour to organize 'sheltered' jobs for crippled and handicapped workers, and a corporation known as 'Remploy' was set up to establish factories in which the disabled could work in suitable conditions.[26] But in spite of these and other services offered by specialized departments, welfare has not become a meaningless and dwindling residue. For here too, as with the children, it has been recognized that the special disability, for the treatment of which a technical expertise is necessary, creates personal and social problems in the sphere of domestic life which are the proper province of a welfare service.

Lastly we come to a category of persons who may be described as those suffering from the most extreme forms of 'social infirmity', prominent among whom are the delinquents, the problem families, and the 'down-and-outs'. Among delinquents it is the treatment of the juveniles that has the strongest social welfare element in it, and we will confine ourselves to them. They are not a class apart, since many of them began life as 'deprived children' or grew up in problem families, or are expressing in the form of delinquency some social or personal trouble which others express in different ways. Today it is the aim of policy to merge the categories and to think, as far as possible, simply in terms of children in trouble. The Juvenile Court, as we have seen, has both to try children charged with an offence and to dispose of those in need of care and protection, and it must treat all those below the age of criminal responsibility (now ten) as falling within the second category. In fact, as a magistrate has expressed it, the Juvenile Court is becoming 'increasingly a clearing house for various social agencies'.[27] The trend here, as in all services with a welfare element, is from the judicial to the social, from the punitive to the helpful, and from confinement in an institution to treatment in the home. Confinement still plays, indeed, an important part in the system in its two relatively modern forms of the Borstal and the Approved School, but it has long been the practice to try first to deal with the case by discharge with a caution, binding over to be of good behavior, or putting on probation. Probation definitely ranks as a welfare service, whatever authority administers it, and owing to its close association with criminal justice it is a peculiarly difficult one to operate. Probation, says one authority, is 'the most advanced application of social case work in the field of criminal justice'.[28]

'Problem family' is a relatively recent term introduced to denote a family so disorganized that it can scarcely be said to function as a family at all. It is likely to contain examples of several kinds of handicap and disability. It is not a very precise category, since it contains a variety of cases, the common feature of which is the need for care and attention of a particularly intensive and continuous kind over a long period. At one time this fell more easily within the province of voluntary agencies than of public authorities, for these lacked the trained staff needed to cope with cases of which one social worker could take on only ten to twelve at a time. It fitted better with the tradition of personal dedication found in the Salvation Army or, later, in the Pacifist Service Units. These were started during the war, and subsequently reconstituted and extended as the Family Service Units. Now these and other voluntary agencies work side by side and in collaboration with the public authorities, both using very much the same methods. These range from preventive measures, to help families which are obviously getting into difficulties, to intensive family case-work in the home, and, by some societies and local councils, to rehabilitation services rendered in special residential quarters. The fact that the work may be undertaken by specially trained home helps, by family counsellors, by home advisers, by welfare officers, or by housing managers underlines the immaturity of social administration in this particular field. The chief difficulty about rehabilitation in special homes is that these can usually take in only the mothers and younger children, and it is impossible to rehabilitate a 'problem family' unless it is kept intact as a unit.[29]

The category of 'problem family' overlaps with that of the homeless, because it contains a high proportion of 'unsatisfactory tenants' likely to be evicted, for non-payment of rent or other causes. The responsibility for sheltering these rests with the welfare departments, though some housing departments employ people to help families in trouble to avoid eviction, or else move them, if they are Council tenants, from the best houses to those of 'intermediate standard' where they can do less damage.[30] But the 'homeless' also include those who have lost their homes for no fault of their own, and those who drift into the cities, especially London, without having any friend or relative who will put them up, or the means to take a furnished lodging even if one could be found. The LCC, which is far harder hit by this problem than any other local authority, had some 3,000 people on its hands by the end of 1961 for whom it had to find short-term accommodation, and the situation was not improving.[31] For these people, too, one of the worst consequences of their predicament is that the family is broken up, and the children may have to be placed 'in care' with the local authority. It is obviously impossible for a housing authority, with a long waiting-list, to let families which have entered the area recently, with no prospects in view, jump the queue for permanent homes.

Quite distinct from the 'problem families' and the temporary homeless are the 'down-and-outs' or homeless vagrants. The responsibility for providing shelter, and such help as is possible, for these people rests on the National Assistance Board, but is generally delegated to the local welfare authorities. Some of the old workhouse casual wards have been converted into Reception Centres where men can lodge for a time and from which some may succeed in getting jobs, and the Board runs three centres for 're-establishing' men who have been unemployed for a long time. The aim is not to give technical training for a job, but to restore morale and the capacity for regular work. But the public services can do but little for the hard core, which includes a high proportion of mental cases, drunkards, and 'meth' addicts, the apathetic who do not trouble even to draw their allowance, and those who are deeply allergic to domestic life. But much help is given to them by the devoted services of workers in voluntary organizations.[32]

Although it has not been possible to do more in this chapter than present the salient features of the welfare services today, enough has been said to show what are the directions of change and the crucial issues of policy in the 1960's. First, in the British system the separation between cash benefits and welfare services has been, on the whole, maintained. The assignment of welfare functions to the Assistance Board in 1940 was a temporary arrangement which really ended when the National Assistance Act (Part III) defined the welfare responsibilities of the local authorities. But one breach has been made in the system by the Children's Act of 1963, which has authorized local Children's Committeee to give help in kind and also, in 'exceptional circumstances', in cash. But the sums involved are small and the purposes for which they may be used peripheral. In the case of old people the separation of cash from service remains in force and, since insurance benefits and assistance allowances are also separated, an old person must collect his pension from the Post Office, his supplementary pension from the National Assistance Board, and apply to the local Welfare Department if he wants a place in a Home. If there were a full-scale superannuation system, which would, of course, be nationally administered, any additional payments could be regarded, not as supplements to the pension, but as an element in the welfare service required to meet exceptional needs, and integrated with it.

But, as some Children's Officers are already feeling, the intrusion of cash into the welfare relationship might contaminate a service which has only recently succeeded in freeing itself from association with poverty; for most people feel that it is more humiliating to accept money than personal service. This is the second general point to note, that poverty has become, in principle, irrelevant to the welfare situation. One must say 'in principle' because most, though by no means all, of those seeking aid from welfare departments are poor, and poverty is one of the causes of their need. But the services are given to all, without question, if the need is real, and only subsequently are they asked how much, if anything, they can pay. Realistic charges are fixed for children in care and old people in Homes, and the clients make a signed declaration of income on the basis of which their contribution is assessed. Very few pay the maximum, and very many the minimum, which, in the case of old people, is the Retirement Pension less pocket-money of about 10s a week. So in the welfare services we find both charges and a means test, and no serious objection to either.

Thirdly, there is the campaign for 'community care', that is to say a system of services rendered by the community, to the community, in the community—which means mostly in the home, but also, when appropriate, in various kinds of local club, centre, or clinic. It is not a precise term or a new idea, and we have seen already how it arose in the case of children and old people. Its role in the health service is a subject that belongs to the next chapter.

The last point to notice is that, in spite of the development of specialized services, the prestige of the welfare service remains high, and is rising. There is a movement to expand and strengthen it, which springs from several sources. It is not so much an attack on the specialized services as a plea to remember that the individual and the family are indivisible units, however much their problems may have to be submitted for diagnosis and treatment to different, technically competent agencies. The scientific analysis of social problems so powerfully advocated by the Webbs was an excellent thing in its day but, as the present author urged in 1946, it needs to be followed by a process of synthesis to re-integrate the social reality which analysis has split into its component parts.[33] Welfare has a key role to play in this process, because it is concerned with the common element present in all cases.

There is also a problem of specialization within the welfare services themselves. Mr Ruck has observed that 'the welfare

services are essentially homogeneous. The fundamental needs of all
human beings, whether handicapped or not, are the same.'[34] But
this has not prevented them from being distributed among a variety
of agencies, both public and private, and among social workers
claiming possession of a variety of skills. The result is sometimes a
degree of duplication which must bewilder the recipients of their
well-meaning attentions. A case is recorded of a family which had
been visited on behalf of at least six public agencies and six voluntary organizations, while its members had spent about a dozen
periods in various institutions.[35]

The easiest answer to this situation is found in the magic word
'co-ordination'. In practice this means either working through
joint committees and case conferences, which are not always a
success, or assigning overall responsibility for a case to the representative of one of the agencies involved, which demands a spirit of
co-operation not always easily engendered. An elaborate scheme
was started in France in 1948 in the Seine Department under a
committee (Conseil de Surveillance) representing all the health and
welfare services, public and private, and the social workers. It
organized a unified family service for each arrondissement. The
staff remained in the employment of their own agencies, but worked
as a team under a designated leader. The plan included an Information Bureau for sorting out cases which resembled in some respects
a Citizens' Advice Bureau, or perhaps even more closely the Family
Bureaux recommended by Mrs Peggy Jay as centres to which
those in need of a family welfare service could come for advice
and help.[36]

This last proposal implies something better described as fusion
than co-ordination, but it refers to centres of information, not to
the services themselves. Complete administrative fusion of these is
hardly possible because, however similar the tasks of the social
workers who deal directly with the clients in their homes, the set-
tings in which the problems arise and must be solved are very
different. The same welfare worker may be able to help a neglected
child, a lonely old woman, a blind man, a cripple, a mental defective,
an unmarried mother, the homeless, or a problem family, but the
responsibilities of those directing the services concerned with these
cases differ profoundly as regards the special knowledge they call for,
the institutions and equipment needed, the outside contacts that
must be cultivated, and the other services whose co-operation must
be enlisted. So the answer to wasteful duplication lies in the

fusion, not of the services as administrative wholes, but of the welfare element common to all of them. It has often been suggested, for instance, that the local authorities should have at their disposal a staff of family case-workers, either distributed among the various departments, like the *Assistantes Sociales* in France, or forming a separate unit of their own to which the various departments could refer their cases.[37]

The Younghusband Working Party (1959) on social workers in the public health and welfare services pursued these questions further. They had been asked in particular to examine the case for the so-called 'general purpose social worker'. It is clear that they were a bit frightened of the idea. For in the first place there was the danger that it might lower the status of many social workers to that of a kind of maid-of-all-work. And secondly it seemed to overstress the common element in welfare work to the point of underestimating the need for specialized skills. So, by a subtle twist, they substituted for the concept of the 'general purpose social worker' that of the 'general purpose function', which can be discharged by social workers at every level—by the fully qualified specialist wherever her high-level skills are needed, by the 'officer with general training in social work' over a very wide range of cases, and by welfare assistants where the services required are of a simpler and more material kind. They could all have a primary attachment to a particular department and a particular type of case, but be available for work outside their special field.[38] There are signs that things are likely to develop along these lines, but no clear pattern has as yet emerged. We shall consider some other aspects of these problems in Chapter 12.

1   M. Penelope Hall, *The Social Services of Modern England* (5th ed.), p. 308
2   S. K. Ruck, *London Government and the Welfare Services*, p. 9
3   Barbara Rodgers and Julia Dixon, *Portrait of Social Work*, p. 31
4   Edith Abbott, *Public Assistance*, vol. I, p. 60
5   Charity Organization Society, *How to Help Cases of Distress*, 1945, p. 18
6   Hansard (Commons), 1947, vol. 444, col. 1608
7   Ruck, op. cit., pp. 33–4
8   K. M. Slack, *Councils, Committees and Concern for the Old*, p. 32
9   Hall, op. cit., p. 307; Ruck, op. cit., p. 38

10   Old Age and Widows Pension Act, 1940, Clause 10(4); Rowntree Committee on 'Old People', p. 14

11   Report of the Assistance Board, 1945, Cmd. 6700, p. 8

12   Kathleen Woodroofe, *From Charity to Social Work*, p. 127

13   Care of Children Committee (Curtis) Report, paras. 63 and 32

14   Hubback Committee, *The Neglected Child and his Family*, pp. 79 and 83

15   Curtis Committee Report, para. 422

16   ibid., para. 439

17   Hubback Committee, op. cit., pp. 105 and 111

18   Children's Department of the Home Office, Report, 1961, p. 2

19   Peter Townsend, *The Last Refuge*, p. 133

20   ibid., p. 511

21   ibid., p. 143

22   Karl Evang, *Health Services in Norway*, p. 114

23   Stanley Alderson, *Britain in the Sixties—Housing*, p. 115

24   J. H. Sheldon, *The Social Medicine of Old Age*, p. 197

25   Margaret N. Hill, *An Approach to Old Age and its Problems*, p. 86

26   Hall, op. cit., pp. 302–5

27   Donald Ford, *The Delinquent Child and the Community*, p. 19

28   Max Grünhut, *Penal Reform*, p. 305

29   A. P. Philp and Noel Timms, *The Problem of the 'Problem Family'*

30   Central Housing Advisory Committee, *Unsatisfactory Tenants*, 1955

31   Alderson, op. cit., p. 111

32   Philip O'Connor, *Britain in the Sixties—Vagrancy*, pp. 64–71 and 80–2

33   T. H. Marshall, *Sociology at the Crossroads and Other Essays*, pp. 8–11

34   Ruck, op cit., p. 122

35   D. V. Donnison, *The Neglected Child and the Social Services*, pp. 72–3

36   Walter A. Friedlander, *Individualism and Social Welfare*, pp. 140–4; Peggy Jay, 'A Plan for Family Bureaux' in *The Ingleby Report— Three Critical Essays*, pp. 11–14

37   Rodgers and Dixon, op. cit., pp. 239–43

38   Report of the Working Party on Social Workers in the Local Authority Health and Welfare Services, 1959, paras. 700–24

10

Health

No modern government can disclaim responsibility for the health of its people, nor would it wish to do so. Policies, therefore, do not differ in the aim pursued, but rather in the methods adopted in pursuit of them. The acceptance of the responsibility does not imply that a government must provide and direct all the services itself, nor that it must offer them free of charge to the whole population. But it must have an overall view of the total volume of resources devoted to the cause of health, of the extent to which the services are available, both geographically and financially, to those in need of them and of their quality, and it must be satisfied with what it sees. And whether a government creates a centrally planned and directed health service, as in the Soviet Union, or gives as much scope as possible to private enterprise and consumer choice, as in the United States, the goal is the same, and the totality of effort expended may be very similar. But the results may differ significantly.

In the less-developed countries, though the possibilities offered by modern medical science and sanitary services are fully appreciated, economic circumstances and social conditions make it necessary to adhere to a standard lower than what is known to be desirable. Policy must be governed by what the country can afford, and scarce resources must be concentrated where the need is judged to be most urgent. But in the more advanced countries it has become apparent in recent years that considerations of cost play only a subsidiary role in the determination of policy. It is quite true that not long ago the rising costs of the British health service were causing much anxiety and provoking some loud protests, and in 1950 the government tried to fix a ceiling above which the total expenditure must not rise. The attempt failed. Then the Guillebaud Committee (1955-6) revealed that the figures generally quoted were misleading. For although the initial cost of the National Health Service was more than double some of the preliminary estimates, and rose steeply in the first five years of operation, the proportion of the Gross National Product absorbed by the service had actually fallen slightly from 3·51% to 3·24%, while the cost per head of the population (at 1948–9 prices) had risen only from £7 13s to £8 12s.[1]

Since then there has been a marked change in attitude and, although costs have continued to rise, nobody seriously proposes that the rate of expenditure should be fixed first, and the standard of service adjusted accordingly. That would be to put the cart before the horse. For in the matter of health, as of education, there are criteria by which a country arrives at a conception of the kind of service that properly belongs to a society at its level of civilization. It is partly a question of fixing a ratio of doctors, nurses, and hospital beds to the population which experience, and comparison with other countries, shows to be acceptable. Then the changing climate of opinion demands amenities and a consideration for the comfort of patients which previous generations would have regarded as unnecessary. As for the treatment itself, it will be remembered that in the inter-war years leading doctors were saying that the benefits of modern medical science were not reaching the people at large. It is now assumed that they must, and that the nation must be able to afford the cost. This is not a precise standard, but it serves.

Although standards may declare themselves in this way in theory, they are often elusive in practice. For the task of devising an organization which will allow every part of the structure to operate to the best advantage is one of formidable difficulty. The trouble is that in the broad area of health and welfare everything is tied up with everything else, and any plan one devises for allocating specific functions to particular organs is bound to sever vital links at many points. The problem is to discover which gaps in the continuity of the system can most easily be bridged by co-operation between the different agencies. The British system is peculiar in that it splits the health services into three distinct parts—public health, general practice, and hospitals—which are not, at any point below the central Ministry, subject to a single administrative authority. But, although much of the criticism of the working of the service is directed to defects due to lack of co-ordination between the three parts, all the official Committees which have studied the matter have advised against their amalgamation. The strongest arguments in support of this position are first that the hospital system must be centrally planned and directed, and based on regions other than those of local Government; secondly, that general practice should not be put under the local councils, because these are not equipped to cope with it, and the doctors would strongly object; and thirdly that the public health side cannot be put under either of the other two sectors, because it must not be detached from the other local services, especially welfare, housing, and education. But the 'Porritt Committee' (1962), representing all branches of the medical profession, thought otherwise. It was so impressed by the defects of the tripartite system and the failure, so far, to co-ordinate the work of its three parts, that it recommended entrusting all the services at the local level (except the Teaching Hospitals) to Area Health Boards in charge of new regions specially designed for the purpose. These Boards would take over the 'social health' functions of the local authorities, but not their welfare services. Unfortunately the Committee did no more than sketch the outlines of their plan, and they made no real attempt to solve the problems which had discouraged their predecessors from making similar proposals for the consolidation of the health services.[2]

The most serious charges made against the service today are that it cuts the general practitioner (GP) off from the main stream of medical progress, which flows through the hospitals and the consulting rooms of specialists, thus pushing him from the centre to the periphery of the stage, and that it lowers the prestige of the local health authority and prevents it from exercising the bene- ficent influence it should over the health and welfare of all members of its community. Taking this second point first, it is easy to under- stand why the Institute of Public Administration should denounce the original act as 'an instrument for the greatest curtailment of local government functions which has taken place for 150 years'.[3] It is not only that the councils were deprived of some of their ex- isting functions, like the management of municipal hospitals, but even more that they have been denied the opportunity of playing the central role in the drama of the future for which their opposite numbers in many other countries were being cast. The first duty assigned to public health had been to prevent illness by protecting the population against dangers inherent in the physical and, to some extent, the human environment. It was concerned with sanitation, water supplies, and slums on the one hand, and with vaccination, immunization and, isolation on the other. Its work came to be overshadowed by the spectacular achievements of curative medicine, and it was said at one time of doctors who went in for public health that they had 'gone to the dogs and the drains'. But when the World Health Organization made its second Report on the World Health situation (published in 1963), it found that environmental improvement topped all other problems in the reports submitted by the Member States. And it was not just a question of drains; the concern was with such things as noise abatement, air pollution, radiation hazards, and the fluoridation of water, and with the possible effects of fertilizers, pesticides, and preservatives.[4] Some of these matters were dealt with at the centre, rather than at the local level, but all belonged to the province of public health.

The other traditional function of public health was to provide certain community services, in or within easy reach of the homes of the people. They now include midwives, district nurses, health visitors, and home helps, as well as clinics of various kinds of which those for expectant and nursing mothers are the most important. The role of these services in the task of co-ordination is obvious. A woman who is going to have a baby is under the care of a general practitioner and may go into hospital for the confinement. But the community health services are at hand throughout, from the beginning of the pregnancy until recuperation is complete, and it is through their contacts among themselves, and with the doctor, the hospital, and the welfare services, that the nature of her various needs can be ascertained and arrangements made to meet them. The value of these services consists not only in what they actually do for the patient, in the way of nursing or domestic work, but also in the information that they gather about the circumstances of the case, and in their function as a vehicle of health education.

Health education occupies a more prominent place in public health programmes today than ever before, because of the growing insistence on the priority to be given to preventive measures, of which it is one. A book on *Recent Advances in Public Health* (1959) lists twenty-six different media which can be used for health education.[5] This certainly bears witness to a lively interest in the subject, but the progress made in actually exploiting these media has been rather slow. Equally important for the prevention of illness is early diagnosis, and the two merge into one another. The following list of some of the principal services offered illustrates the point: the medical inspection of school children, mass X-ray examinations, pre- and post-natal clinics, child welfare centres, the campaign against venereal disease, instruction to diabetics on diet and the use of insulin, and general propaganda about healthy living, including in recent times warnings about the connection between smoking and lung cancer.

But the key institution through which the local authority was to exercise its greatest power of co-ordination, the Health Centre, has not materialized in the form in which it was originally envisaged. It was to be a place where general practitioners and specialists came together under the aegis of the local authority to carry on their normal work, and where, in addition, the community health services would be located or have their base. There is nothing extravagant about the idea, for it has been adopted as a vital part of the health system in many countries, especially in the form of polyclinics in rural areas or of out-patient departments in places which cannot afford full-scale hospitals.[6] The author of the book just mentioned lamented that whereas there were 30,000 poly-clinics in the USSR there were only seventeen centres in the United Kingdom.[7] The fact is that the Health Centre fits easily into a system in which the various branches of the service are amalgam-ated, and directed by a single comprehensive authority in each area. But it did not fit into the British tripartite structure; the local authorities found it was beyond their powers to create so complex an organization, and the doctors did not want to become so de-pendent on the local authorities. So the original enthusiasm for Health Centres waned rather rapidly, and although some inter-esting experiments have been, and are being, made, Health Centres have not become a regular feature of the service.

So far as the organization of general practice is concerned their place has been taken by partnerships and group practices. Only about a quarter of the GP's now work alone, and even these must have a 'rota system' by which neighbouring colleagues can relieve them. For they are under an obligation to provide a service for twenty-four hours a day, seven days a week, and fifty-two weeks a year. The ideal partnership, according to Dr Stephen (later Lord) Taylor, is composd of four or five doctors who pool their expenses and receipts, but retain their own lists of patients, helping each other out when necessary.[8] Group practice proper implies a single, common list of patients; it allows for some specialization within the range of general practice and the provision of some of the more expensive equipment. The doctors can work to a timetable and so get time off for study or to take a session at a hospital. In order to help doctors to meet the initial cost of setting up a group practice, the government established a fund in 1953 to grant interest-free loans for this purpose.

But all this has not been enough to allay the discontent that was widely felt among GP's when they saw how the system was operating. Some of their earlier protests about their rate of remuneration were met by adjustment of the scales, but discontent has persisted, and in fact become more vocal. Their main complaints are, or have been, that they are overworked and underpaid, that there is no relation between the quality of the service they give and the remuneration that they receive, that, with a full list, they cannot give enough time and attention to their patients, that a free service encourages people to make unnecessary visits to, and demands on, their doctor, that they have no direct access to the most modern methods of diagnosis and must send all the interesting cases to the hospital out-patient department, and that once their patient has entered a hospital for treatment they lose all contact with him.

One of these charges has been shown by Professor Titmuss to have been unjustified, at least when it was first made. For the statistics indicate that patients did not increase their visits to the surgery, or their calls for the doctor to visit them, after the National Health Service came into operation.[9] Others of the complaints cannot be laid at the door of the service, but are the natural results of developments in the science and practice of medicine. Nevertheless the remainder, which are definitely criticisms of the way the service is organized, are serious and mostly well founded, as can be seen from the Report of the Gillie Committee of 1963, which is much less complacent in tone than some of its predecessors. Capitation fees, say the doctors, are so low that many of them have to enrol patients up to, or near to, the permitted maximum (now 3,500) in order to make a decent living. And every doctor interviewed by the Gillie Committee 'regretted the impossibility of achieving a satisfying standard of work with the present maximum under existing working conditions'.[10] The doctors are also now objecting that the capitation system means that the efficient doctor earns no more than the inefficient, or the hardworking than the lazy. Hospital consultants are not only better paid, but there are 'merit awards', some of them of very considerable amounts, added to the salaries of the more distinguished. The GP's at one time definitely rejected the idea of 'merit awards' as being invidious, but opinion has veered towards having some method of rewarding competence, diligence, and experience.

The crucial question is, should the capitation system of payment be retained? There are two alternatives, a salaried service, to which most doctors still object, or piece-rate payments for services rendered. The latter would adjust earnings to the volume and character of the work done, but should there then be different rates for the same service as rendered by a more or a less distinguished practitioner? One sees that the system might become complicated and that a financial element would insinuate itself between the doctor and his individual patient. In many countries where piece-rate remuner- ation is the rule the patient pays a percentage of the cost of each service. In France the procedure has been to reimburse 80% of the standard fee. But since, in spite of local agreements between insur- ance committees and doctors' associations to fix standard rates, the doctors could charge what they liked, the reimbursement was often ludicrously inadequate. In 1958, and again in 1960, the government made determined efforts to put things straight by making regional rates effective and providing a national scale for use where no local agreement existed. But it still found it necessary to allow exceptions. So (as an international journal phrased it—in slightly peculiar English) 'fees exceeding the limits fixed are allowed only for the following motives: status of wealth of the insured per- son, standing of the physician and other special circumstances'.[11] The loophole seems to be a very large one, and there may be bargains, disputes, and appeals about the doctor's bill. But these troubles are not the inevitable accompaniment of a system of piece- rates and reimbursement of fees, for they do not seem to be present in such countries as Norway and Sweden, both of which have a system of this kind.

Conditions of work, pay and, of course, training are the main factors determining the quantity and quality of doctors at the dis- posal of the population. The second requirement of any health service is that the doctors should be well and fairly distributed over the country. And here the British system of panels of registered patients and payment by capitation fees has certain advantages. The capitation fee system makes the registration of patients nec- essary, and the lists of registered patients, deposited with the Exe- cutive Councils, provide information by which to judge how the distribution is working, as well as a basis for exercising some control

over it. The right of doctors working in the national service to buy
and sell practices was abolished by the Act of 1946. Areas in which
supply and demand are not satisfactorily balanced are classified
as either over-doctored or under-doctored. Doctors are not allowed
to establish new practices in the former, and some inducements
are offered to persuade them to settle in the latter. The result can
be seen in the decline in the percentage of all patients in under-
doctored (or 'designated') areas from 51·5 in 1952 to 17·6 in 1962.[12]
Distribution is less satisfactory in countries where there are no
panels, and anybody can go to any doctor at any time. In Norway,
for instance, the Director General of the Health Services has admitted that the freedom allowed to both patients and doctors
'results in uneven distribution of doctors over the country'.[13]

The complaints of the GP's which arise from the progess of
medicine rather than the defects of the system all relate to the shift
of the centre of gravity to the hospitals, where high-grade specialists
work with modern techniques and equipment, leaving the general
practitioner out in the cold. It was with this problem in view that
the Gillie Committee was asked to advise on the role of the 'family
doctor' in the health service, as it would be likely to develop in the
next ten to fifteen years. It is an odd formulation, since the term
'family doctor' went out of fashion many years ago, and it was
generally believed that the species was extinct, if, indeed, it had
ever really existed except among the relatively small class of well-
to-do families. So the Committee's task was not only forward-
looking, but also a creative one. It had to see how to resuscitate
the family doctor first, before it could assign him his role.

The essential feature of family doctoring is that one man has
continuous care of a whole family, and gets to know it through and
through. In this respect the National Health Service is an advance
on its predecessor, National Health Insurance, because the latter
did not cover the dependants of the insured, whereas in the present
system all members of the family normally go to the same doctor.
And secondly the family doctor should enjoy the full confidence of
the family as a repository of up-to-date medical knowledge, and have
the authority necessary for the issue of 'doctors' orders'. Today
he only too often does not. It is partly because his patients know
too much, thanks to the spread of health education by radio,
television, and other media, and they have been impressed by the
contrast between the miracles worked in hospitals and the hum-
drum business that goes on in the doctor's surgery. But it is mainly

because, whether the patients demand it or not, the GP is bound to pass a high proportion of his cases on to the specialist and the hospital.

Group practice increases the range of services the GP can offer, but it may do so at the expense of undermining his character as a family doctor, since the various members of the family may see different members of the group, according to the nature of their complaint. The obvious way of keeping doctors up-to-date is by training, and much thought has been given to ways of improving this. Refresher courses are run in graduate medical schools, and 3,500 doctors attended them in 1961–2. There are three main ways of bridging the gap between the family doctor and the hospital. It would be very difficult to provide regular opportunities for transfer between the two branches of the profession, but it is rather easier to arrange for GP's to work part-time as members of a hospital staff. Some 6,000 salaried posts of this kind were filled by family doctors in 1962.[14] Secondly hospital consultants can undertake domiciliary visits to the family doctor's patients. It has been the policy to encourage this practice, and in 1962 some 300,000 such visits were recorded. But unfortunately the link forged in this way was less strong than it might have been, since in more than half the cases the doctor was not there when the consultant called.[15] Finally hospitals may contain a certain number of 'general practitioner beds' in which the GP can treat his patients within the hospital walls, as has always been the practice in the small cottage hospitals.

In January 1962 the government produced its great hospital plan, under which an eventual total of £700 million would be spent on expansion and improvement. Its central feature is the District General Hospital to be sited in such of the larger towns in each region as are not already major hospital centres. These are to contain paediatric, geriatric, maternity and psychiatric units, isolation wards and up-to-date out-patient departments, in fact everything except some of the more highly specialized services. The local doctors will be able to send patients to them for diagnostic tests without having to go through one of the hospital medical staff, which is an important advance on present procedures. And there will also be some 'general practitioner beds' in them, but only for cases which could have been treated at home if domestic conditions had been better and the necessary nursing could have been provided. And such cases ought to decline in number if 'community care' means anything. In addition some of the smaller hospitals which the District General Hospitals will replace may be converted into clinics of various kinds, or into out-patient departments. All this may lead to a better organized institutional service, but it is not yet clear that it will notably improve the status or markedly change the role of the family doctor.[16]

It is interesting to compare this plan with the system described by an international team which recently visited the Soviet Union under the auspices of the World Health Organization. There too the key institution is the regional hospital, carefully sited, but its functions are much wider. It contains within itself the direction of all the regional health services, and spreads its influence far and wide through a network of local clinics and health centres with the result, says the report, that the health services now 'reach every home even in the most remote and isolated localities'.[17] But what one notices is the absence of any reference to the family doctor, or even to domiciliary visits of any kind. A similar tendency for the doctor to enter the home only in order to send the patient to hospital is found in other countries, including the United States. But this highly institutionalized structure is in sharp contrast with the British concept of 'community care'.

But, one may ask, what does that concept really amount to? In the case of welfare, as we have seen, it involves a projection and consolidation of trends which have been operating for some time. But in the case of health the trend has been on the whole in the opposite direction and has to be reversed. The government's hospital development plan is based on the assumption that 'the first concern of the health and welfare services will continue to be to forestall illness and disability by preventive measures', while for those who fall sick 'the aim will be to provide care at home and in the community for all who do not require the special types of diagnosis and treatment which only a hospital can provide'.[18] It is remarkable that the most massive hospital development plan of modern times should be prefaced by a statement asserting the priority, in the health service as a whole, of public health and the family doctor, and one wonders whether the implications have been fully realized. The family doctor has been languishing, and must be resuscitated; old people and mental cases have been demanding more and more hospital beds, and the numbers must be reduced; more and more sick people, especially children, have been brought unnecessarily into the hospitals for treatment, and in future such cases must be kept at home. In order to achieve this it may be necessary, not merely to strengthen the staffs of existing departments, as is mostly the case in the welfare services, but to do some fresh thinking about the types of trained worker required and the departments to which they should be attached.

It was with special reference to mental health that Professor Titmuss recently asked whether community care was 'fact or fiction'. 'In the public mind,' he said, 'the aspirations of reformers are transmuted, by the touch of a phrase, into hard-won reality. What some hope will one day exist is suddenly thought by many to exist already.' But in fact more and more mentally sick persons are being discharged, not as cured, but as 'relieved', and subnormal cases are handed over for supervision in the community before there are enough people able and ready to look after them.[19]

We should, however, remember that the mental health services have had a chequered career. Back in 1913 the stress had been on procedures for classifying and confining those not considered fit to be at large, and the mental hospitals were administered by the local authorities under the direction of the central Board of Control. Between the wars the attitude changed, thanks largely to the devoted work of some voluntary organizations and to the advances made in psychiatric medicine. The Royal Commission of 1924–6 laid it down that no sharp line of demarcation should be drawn between mental and physical illness; the two should be treated alike. 'The keynote of the past has been detention. The keynote of the future should be prevention and treatment.'[20] So after the war the mental hospitals were transferred from the Board of Control and the local authorities to the Minister of Health and his hospital system, as an integral part of the new National Health Service. In 1959, however, policy was redefined in an Act described by the Ministry of Health as 'a major event in the history of the health services',[21] which declared that first priority should be given to treatment at home, second to residential hostels, and third priority only to mental hospitals. So the local authorities found themselves charged once more with a large part of the responsibility of which they had only recently been relieved, and they set to work to establish hostels for the mentally afflicted and training centres for the mentally subnormal about as fast as their limited resources permitted. Meanwhile the hospital service was moving into the area of community care from its side by setting up 'day hospitals', where psychiatric patients, infirm old people and the physically handicapped could receive care and treatment while continuing to sleep at home. The

distinction between these and day centres run by welfare departments, says one writer, 'is a matter of theory rather than practice'.[22]

The degree to which a country can be said to have a national
health service, conceived and functioning as a unity, depends very
much on how the services are financed. There are three possible
sources of revenue—taxation, social insurance, and the personal
incomes of the patients.

Where medical care is an insurance benefit one usually finds that
the scheme does not cover the whole population, that entitlement
to benefit must be established by evidence of contributions paid,
that the insured have to bear a not inconsiderable part of the cost,
and very often there is a limit to the length of time for which the
service is provided. The tendency of late has been to reduce all these
restrictions, and in particular the time limit, which was abolished
in Norway in 1953 and in France in 1955. But the characteristic
features of an insurance contract have not disappeared.[23] A service
financed from taxes is free of these encumbrances and can more
easily be made comprehensive in the two senses of covering the
whole population and meeting all needs.

Modern medical treatment is expensive, and the less well-to-do
cannot pay for themselves out of their own income or savings. A
comprehensive national service must therefore contain an element
of income redistribution between the richer and the poorer. This is
present if a service, offering the same benefit to all, is financed out
of taxation that is either progressive or proportionate to income. It
is also present if the service, being the same for all, is financed from
insurance contributions assessed as a percentage of earnings, a
procedure widely followed today, but rejected by Beveridge as
violating the basic principles of insurance. Where charges are made
for services or commodities at the same rate for all, regardless of
their incomes, they weaken the redistributive element, since they
are a regressive type of levy. But such charges can be remitted for
those who can ill afford to pay them (and generally they are), and
this strengthens the redistributive element again. Payment by the
patients of a proportion of the cost of medical services, both in and
out of hospital, is a feature of many insurance systems. Payment of
a part, or even the whole, of the cost of medicines and appliances
is still commoner, being found also in services financed out of taxes,
like the British, and even in Communist countries such as Poland,
Hungary, and the USSR.[24] No social principle seems to be involved,
the aim being simply to reduce the burden falling on the taxpayer.

The whole picture is quite different in the United States, the one large and highly developed country that does not have a national health service in the sense in which we are using the term. It is true that large sums are spent by the Federal, State, and local governments on public health, on the medical care of certain categories of person (public servants, veterans, the 'needy sick' and so forth), and on medical training and research, and many hospitals and clinics are run by public authorities. Nevertheless, the United States offers the best example of a medical profession jealously guarding its independence almost at any cost,* and of the use of voluntary insurance as the principal organized way of meeting the family's medical bills. It is hard to think of any other country in which a proposal to give medical care to the aged as an insurance benefit would be denounced, and defeated, as an attempt 'to bring socialized medicine to the nation through the back door'.[25] The risk most widely covered by voluntary insurance is the basic cost of a stay in hospital, and the largest society offering this kind of policy is Blue Cross. Next comes the cost of surgical treatment, with Blue Shield as the principal agency, and last, as a very bad third, come physicians' fees. It may be that two-thirds of the population have some sort of medical insurance, but the distribution is uneven. The proportion is high (up to 80%) in the middle income-group, but low among the poorer classes of the community. And those who can afford to pay only moderate premiums are likely to recover only about one-third of their costs.[26] A survey of old people who had gone to hospital showed that 28% of them consumed more than half their savings, many were left with unpaid debts, and most of them had to beg help from friends and relatives.[27]

The defects of the voluntary insurance system have been frankly stated by American experts. It tends to concentrate on curative treatment and to ignore prevention and early diagnosis. It excludes certain types of illness, such as tuberculosis and mental ailments, and does very little to ease the financial burden of either 'catastrophic' or chronic illness.[28] That is why a Presidential Commission in 1952–3 recommended the expenditure of another billion dollars 'to make tuberculosis, mental disease, and chronic illness facilities available to the entire population without a means test'.[29] This has not yet been done. The area of greatest progress has been the hospital service. In 1948 a Presidential enquiry showed that the country had less than half the hospital beds it needed. Legislation followed

* The strike of Belgian doctors occurred after this sentence was written

authorizing Federal subsidies to State programmes of hospital building, with the result that it was said in 1960 that the number of hospital beds had risen to 80% of requirements. And, according to the World Health Organization, this great American effort helped to stimulate a similar and equally determined effort in Europe 'to renovate the whole hospital scene'.[30]

Many voices have been prophesying that the growing sense of public responsibility for health in the United States will lead to the establishment of some form of national health service. At a Conference in 1954 one speaker said that the 'snail-pace evolution' of medical insurance must 'increase public pressure for government intervention in financing general medical care'.[31] A Professor of Public Health, writing in 1964, declared that 'American medicine is gradually proceeding along the same general course toward a systematic national organization of health services as one may see in Great Britain, Scandinavia, New Zealand, the Soviet Union, Chile, and elsewhere'.[32] And Gunnar Myrdal, at about the same date, wrote that 'it goes without saying that America cannot postpone much longer a comprehensive system of pensions for invalids and of health insurance'. Voluntary insurance, however much it might expand, was not enough.[33]

There is little likelihood, therefore, that Britain will, in the foreseeable future, take the advice of those who wish to move towards the American model by charging patients as much as they can afford to pay for all services, and leaving them to cover the cost, as far as they can, by voluntary insurance. To do so would be to violate the basic principles of the National Health Service as conceived by Aneurin Bevan, namely that no element of commercialism should enter between doctor and patient, and that illness is neither an indulgence for which people ought to pay nor an offence for which they should be penalized, but a misfortune the cost of which should be shared by the community. Some extension of the range of things for which a fixed minimum charge is made is not out of the question, but it should be noted that when, in July 1964, the British Medical Association declared that it might not object to making patients pay for consulting their family doctor, this idea was quickly repudiated in the House of Commons by the spokesman of the two major political parties.

The real issue today is a rather different one, namely the proper place of private practice in a society that has a national service. The Porritt Committee thought it important that private practice should flourish, because it provides 'an incentive and a stimulus' to the medical profession and 'affords a valuable contrast and comparison to the health service'. Without it the State service would become a monopoly, which would be 'disastrous'.[34] The argument is not a very convincing one, because so many of the advantages obtained by those who pay for themselves are precisely the things that cannot be given to everybody. Everybody cannot have a private room in a hospital, and you cannot eliminate a queue by allowing some people to jump it. Nobody, however, seriously proposes to suppress private practice, and it can, no doubt, have a stimulating effect, especially if it helps to attract recruits to the profession. The question is whether it should be positively encouraged, and that depends very much on the measures by which the encouragement might be given.

One way is to increase the number and lower the price of private rooms in hospitals and nursing homes. Another, and a more far-reaching one, is to ease the financial burden of those who choose to pay for themselves so that private practice would have more customers. This could be done by allowing them to 'opt out' of the State scheme, which means that their contributions to the cost of that scheme (through taxation and compulsory insurance) would be remitted and could be invested in private insurance. An alternative, preferred by the Porritt Committee, is to allow a rebate of income tax on voluntary medical insurance contributions and to subsidize the private insurance organizations. The Committee defended this suggestion on the grounds that the growth of private practice would reduce the cost of the public services. But it is difficult to see how this could happen to any significant extent, since the State would have to continue to offer the same range of services to a smaller number of people, which does not sound like a very economical proposition. The danger is that any scheme for boosting private practice would have a depressing rather than a stimulating effect on the public service, and might lead to what Bevan called 'a two standard health service, one below and one above the salt'. But these are matters on which final judgement must be reserved to some future date.

Meanwhile the British National Health Service, with all its faults, is an outstanding achievement, as foreign observers have frankly admitted. 'Careful study', says the author of the latest American book on it, 'makes it clear that the British people have done incredibly well.'[35] And, judging by the Gallup Poll carried out for the Porritt Committee, the British people are of the same mind. The Committee, in fact, 'had no difficulty in reaching the conclusion that, basically, the concept of a comprehensive national health service is sound'.[36] It was not even seriously pessimistic about the status and prospects of the general practitioner. The only major defect it found in the service, apart from its tripartite administrative structure, was the failure to do enough forward planning, and that is a natural fault in the second decade of the life of a great experiment, when there is every temptation to take a rest after the immense effort and expense of its initiation.

1   Committee of Enquiry into the Cost of the National Health Service (Guillebaud Committee), 1955-6, p. 9; B. Abel Smith and R. M. Titmuss, *The Cost of the National Health Service*, p. 60

2   A Review of the Medical Services in Great Britain; Report of the Medical Services Review Committee (Porritt Report), 1962, pp. 22-5

3   J. M. Mackintosh, *Trends of Opinion about the Public Health*, p. 167

4   World Health Organization, Second Report on the World Health Situation, 1962, pp. 19-20 and 45

5   J. L. Burn, *Recent Advances in Public Health*, p. 110

6   WHO, First Report on the World Health Situation, 1959, p. 135

7   Burn, op. cit., p. 81

8   Stephen Taylor, *Good General Practice*, pp. 92-3

9   R. M. Titmuss, *Essays on the Welfare State*, p. 174

10 The Field of Work of the Family Doctor (Gillie Report), 1963, pp. 33-6

11 Bulletin of the International Social Security Association, April 1959, p. 167

12 Ministry of Health, Report for 1958, p. 92, and for 1962, p. 42

13 Karl Evang, *Health Services in Norway*, p. 27

14 Ministry of Health, Report for 1962, pp. 45 and 105

15 Gillie Report, p. 31

16 Ministry of Health, *A Hospital Plan for England and Wales*, 1962

17 WHO Health Services in the USSR (Public Health Papers no. 3), 1960, p. 11

18 Ministry of Health, *A Hospital Plan . . .* , p. 9

19 R. M. Titmuss, 'Community Care—Fact or Fiction?' in H. Freeman and J. Farndale (ed.), *Trends in the Mental Health Services*, p. 221

20 Kathleen Jones, *Mental Health and Social Policy*, pp. 109-10

21 Ministry of Health, Report for 1959, p. 6

22 Freeman and Farndale, op. cit., pp. 69 and 177-86

23 ILO, The Cost of Medical Care, 1959, pp. 23-52

24 US Department of Health, Education and Welfare, *Social Security Programs throughout the World*, 1961

25 V. D. Bornet, *Welfare in America*, p. 308

26 Oscar N. Serbein, *Paying for Medical Care in the United States passim*; O. W. Anderson and J. J. Feldman, *Family Medical Costs and Voluntary Health Insurance*, pp. 25 and 14

27 US Department of Health, Education and Welfare, *The Impact of Hospitalization on Aged Beneficiaries* (Highlight Report no. 6), pp. 3–6

28 Serbein, op. cit., pp. 179–80 and 353

29 J. E. Russell (ed.), *National Policies for Education, Health and Social Services*, p. 215

30 America's Health—Report of the National Health Assembly, pp. 40–3; WHO First Report on the World Health Situation, p. 33

31 William Haber in Russell, op. cit., p. 187

32 William I. Roemer, 'Free Enterprise in Medicine' in *New Society*, 9 January 1964, p. 13

33 Gunnar Myrdal, *Challenge to Affluence*, p. 63

34 Porritt Report, p. 32

35 Almont Lindsey, *Socialized Medicine in England and Wales*, p. xi

36 Porritt Report, p. 14

11

Housing

Housing may legitimately be included in a study of social policy for several reasons. Homelessness, and living conditions which destroy or gravely endanger health, are matters to which no government can be indifferent. This determines the minimum responsibility which all modern governments must accept. How much further their responsibility should extend towards the ultimate maximum of ensuring that every family has a home 'fit for heroes'—or for respectable citizens—to live in is open to debate. For standards rise all the time, and it is hard to keep up with them. In discharging their responsibility, however defined, governments have for some time past intervened, or interfered, in the operation of the market economy on the grounds that the economy, left to itself, was not providing all that the governments considered necessary for social welfare. And this, as has been apparent in every chapter of this book, is a characteristic feature of social policy. But it does not follow that housing must necessarily be treated as a social service, though it may be, and some people think that it should be.

We are accustomed to distinguish between the social services and the public utilities, like gas and electricity, which, though publicly controlled, are run as commercial enterprises. But recently heated arguments about the operation of the railways have made it clear that the distinction between the two categories is not an obvious one, and that there may be border-line cases containing some of the qualities of both. Housing is one of these cases. It is quite possible for a housing policy to find room at the same time for unfettered private enterprise, for private enterprise subject to public controls, and for public enterprise; and the latter may be administered either as a public utility or as a social service. Differences between one housing policy and another result from differences in the ways in which these various ingredients are used and combined.

Housing is probably the most elusive and intractable of all the problems with which social policy has to deal. It is not easy to measure even the present need for houses. House-room is a peculiarly elastic commodity. In times of shortage people manage to make do with what they have got. They stay in small homes after their families have outgrown them, and young couples begin their married life in a room in a parental house although they would much prefer to have a home of their own. The volume and urgency of such concealed demand are difficult to estimate. One cannot arrive at a conclusion about the need for houses by setting the total number of rooms in the country against the total population. For houses, once they have been built, are immovable and cannot follow shifting demand; so the geographical distribution of living-rooms does not coincide with that of people to live in them. And even within one locality the proportion of rooms per person (or of persons per room) differs greatly from house to house. Over-crowding and under-occupation may exist side by side. The 1961 census showed 'houses and households just about in balance overall though unevenly distributed';[1] there were, by then, enough houses in the country as a whole, but there was at the same time a serious housing shortage in many areas.

When one turns from an estimate of present needs to one of future needs, the calculation becomes still more difficult. It is not simply a matter of allowing for the increase in the population, since the magnitude of the demand for homes depends on its age composition and social structure. If people marry young and have small families the number of household units per 1,000 people will be relatively large, as compared with a society in which people marry later and have larger families, as commonly occurred in the nineteenth century. As the expectation of life of the elderly increases, the turnover rate for houses is reduced, as the older generation remains for longer in occupation of dwellings for which the younger generation is waiting. And there is also an increased demand for a special type of accommodation to suit the aged, especially if an effective policy of 'community care' enables more of them to live at home. A high divorce rate, too, creates a demand for more dwellings by splitting one household into two, until the divorced remarry. But the most difficult factor to assess and allow for is probably the geographical shift of the population, or internal migration. It is possible to exert an influence over this by controlling the siting of factories, offices, and other places of employment, but experience shows that it is not at all easy to exercise this kind of control with sufficient firmness and foresight to secure and maintain a satisfactory regional distribution of houses. It has recently become the fashion in England to use Disraeli's phrase the 'two nations' to refer, not to the rich and the poor, but to the North and the South. The steady drift of industry and population southwards has gone so far that plans have been prepared for large-scale urban development in the South-Eastern counties to absorb the influx.

On the supply side the situation is dominated by two facts. First, houses are a durable commodity with a life of around a hundred years, and the initial capital needed to build one is more than the majority of would-be consumers possess. But their demand can nevertheless become effective if they are enabled to substitute payments out of income for the outlay of capital. This means that they must either borrow the capital at interest and gradually repay it (if possible), or else rent a house either from a landlord whose capital is invested in housing for profit or from a public authority which provides houses in discharge of its statutory obligations. None of these processes can fairly be said to be 'trouble-free'. Secondly there are limits to the speed at which houses can be built. Not only is the actual process of construction a relatively slow one, although techniques of prefabrication and mass production are constantly being improved, but labour and materials cannot be assigned to a national housing programme without regard to other claims for a share in these scarce resources. It must be remembered, too, that the replacement of obsolete houses and the clearance of slums may be, in terms of social welfare, an even more urgent task than that of building to increase the total stock of houses. A housing programme must be prepared to destroy as well as to create, and those evicted in the process have the highest priority among claimants for the new houses that are being built. So, once a serious housing shortage has developed (as it did after both world wars), it is extremely difficult to wipe it out and at the same time to meet a growing demand.

To sum up: the task of housing policy is to estimate as accurately as possible the present and future demand for houses, to wrestle with the physical problems of production, and to manipulate the financial circumstances governing supply and demand as far as is necessary to ensure that houses are made available as fast as the state of the national economy permits, of the kind that the population desires, in the places where they are going to be wanted, and at prices that the people can afford to pay. And in doing this it must have regard to the liberty of the individual, the rights of property, and the principles of social justice. It is not surprising that success in so formidable an undertaking should have proved hard to come by.

We have already reviewed the problems that claimed attention after the First World War, and the policies that were adopted to meet them, and we saw that some of the measures introduced at that time to cope with what was thought to be a temporary emergency were still in force twenty years later. Then came the Second World War, which revived all the problems created by the First, but in a more acute form. Not only did building cease, but vast numbers of houses were destroyed both in Britain and in some of the countries of Europe, especially Germany. In the boom conditions of the post-war revival the cost of building went steadily up, and land values rocketed in the areas of rapid development. At the same time, in the atmosphere of the Welfare State, the level of expectation and the sense of obligation to satisfy it both rose. But the ingredients of which housing policies were compounded remained essentially the same as before the war—subsidies, cheap loans, tax relief, rent restrictions, and rent allowances. Nobody came to the rescue with any new ideas, unless one were to count as such the British initiative in the creation of New Towns. The difference between the various national policies were caused, rather, by the different ways in which the old devices were employed. Speaking very generally, one might hazard the opinion that in Britain housing policy has been more deeply enmeshed in the wrangles of party politics, that housing legislation is more complicated, and that administration is more fussy and paternal than in most of the countries of continental Europe.

Looking at the situation from the angle of demand, one may first note that the trend towards early marriage continues and, combined with a growing desire for independence among the young, increases the ideal ratio of dwellings to total population. At the same time the population is growing faster, as the birth-rate rises and the death-rate falls. In addition, immigration from Commonwealth countries, which was not subject to any restrictions, swelled the number of those seeking homes and, in some cases, created problems of a special kind. The most serious was that caused by the immigrants from the West Indies who flowed in in a steady stream and tended to concentrate in the areas already occupied by

their fellow-countrymen, in overcrowded furnished lodgings where
they were exposed to exploitation by landlords. A not insignificant
part of the trouble about overcrowding and extortionate rents in
London and some other places arose in this way. This was one of
the reasons that induced the government, in 1962, to pass a highly
controversial Act 'to make temporary provision for controlling the
immigration into the United Kingdom of Commonwealth citizens'.
It empowered officials to refuse admission (or permit it for a limited
period only) to those who were not either genuine students, financially self-supporting, or provided with a Ministry of Labour permit
to work. But the problem still remains, and it is as much one of
quality as of quantity. For very many of the immigrants are obliged
to live in conditions which make it harder than ever for them to
adjust themselves to the way of life of the society of which they
have become members, a society which is, in the matter of housing,
striving to raise the general standard to the level of the best.

In trying to improve the quality of housing, it is difficult to decide
how far policy should follow the popular taste and how far it should
set out to lead and to form it. For one thing it is no easy matter to discover what people really want, because most of them cannot judge
whether they would like a particular kind of dwelling until they
have tried it. It used to be assumed that the average British family
preferred a house to a flat, and would rather own than rent it. The
desire to own is certainly very strong, but the habit of flat-dwelling
has spread rapidly in recent years at all social levels, and the old stereo-
type must be amended. Modern design has rendered obsolete many
of the ideas about the kind of life that a block of flats imposes on
its inmates. In a big redevelopment area in Sheffield, says an ob-
server, 'horizontal "streets" meander at every third-floor level,
being bridged from block to block, for over half a mile',[2] and the
visitor to Rio de Janeiro will be struck by the sight of children
rampaging around in an open-air playground, sheltered from the
sun, high above the street.

Then we may find that desires in some cases are contradictory or
self-defeating. A family may think it does not want to live in a flat,
but it may be equally unwilling to move out to a housing estate
which is the only place where, with the present pressure on urban
land, a house can possibly be offered. But here too we should
beware of jumping to conclusions about the real nature, or the
strength, of people's wishes, especially if they are based on out-of-
date stereotypes, such as that which depicts a housing estate as an

arid waste of social segregation; for it is not necessarily anything of the kind. Their investigation of family life in Bethnal Green led Michael Young and P. Willmott to the conclusion that 'very few people wish to leave the East End. They are attached to Mum and Dad, to the markets, to the pubs and settlements, to Club Row and the London Hospital'.[3] But is it doubtful whether this can be accepted as a valid generalization. A similar study by J. B. Cullingworth of people who had moved from Salford to Worsley gave rather different results. Though half the families that moved said they did not want to do so, only 17% subsequently wished to return. And they were not influenced so much by their ties with the old town, or with Mum and Dad, as by dislike of the longer journey to work.[4] This does not make it any easier for the authorities in big cities to solve the problem of where to 'decant their overspill', and often they are not helped at all by what their predecessors have done. For in the first decade or so after the war, says one writer, 'houses anywhere, at once, were preferred to houses in the right place five years ahead',[5] and that sort of behaviour is likely to leave an intractable legacy to those who follow.

The situation on the supply side is dominated by the fact that, to quote Professor Sauvy, 'the building for profit of rentable workers' homes belongs to the past'.[6] The cost of a new house of the required standard of quality is now too high. So, not only are new houses of this kind not being built for letting by private enterprise, but when rented houses fall vacant many of them are sold to owner-occupiers to the extent, according to a recent British survey, of 22%.[7] Houses for letting must therefore be built mainly by public authorities or other non-profit-making agencies. Even then, however, it is generally assumed that it will not be possible to offer the houses at rents low enough to meet the demand, unless financial help is provided in the form either of subsidies or of loans on terms more favourable than those obtainable in the open market.

But is this assumption warranted? The answer depends on what proportion of the family budget should properly be absorbed by rent, and that is a matter not of fact, but of opinion. It is related, for one thing, to changes in the standard of living. It is well known that, as real income rises, the proportion spent on food falls and that which is available to pay for things formerly considered as luxuries rises. There has been, during the present century, a similar tendency for the proportion devoted to housing to fall. On the basis of enquiries by the Ministry of Labour it appears that the figures for British wage-earners was about 15% before the First World War and about 13% shortly before the Second. In the 1950's it was down to less than 7% for unfurnished flats and houses.[8] The figure for working-class rents in general in Sweden at that time was 17% and it had been 35% before the war.[9] Obviously the conception of what a family can afford to pay is a very elastic one. But these are average figures, which conceal a wide range of diversity in individual cases. Nevertheless they do seem to indicate that, in general, housing policy, with its rent restriction and subsidies, had succeeded in keeping rents in general down to a lower level than was really necessary. They do not, however, imply that new houses could now be built without subsidy and let at rents which all but a minority of families could reasonably be expected to pay. The averages are low because of the high proportion of old houses erected when building was much cheaper than it is today. The government's plans to encourage unsubsidized, non-profit building for letting (as described in 1963) envisage a range of houses whose cost (including rates) would be equivalent to from a quarter to nearly a half of the average earnings of a manual worker in industry.[10] It is clear that they must be intended for higher income-groups than this.

The same is true of the houses built for sale to owner-occupiers by unaided private enterprise. But they have an important role to play in the general programme, partly because of the widespread desire in many sections of the population to own their own homes, and partly because of the large contribution they can make to the total stock of houses, without involving public authorities in a lot of administrative work or any direct responsibility beyond that of overall planning. And this contribution can be increased, and extended to lower income-groups, if the policy includes measures to help and encourage private enterprise to invest its capital in this way. The commonest methods used for this purpose are loans on specially favourable terms, tax remission, and even, if the prevailing political philosophy permits this, outright subsidies.

In comparing the housing policies of the various countries of Europe, one must bear in mind their different experiences during the war. Germany suffered the greatest physical destruction, and was thereby stimulated to make the greatest effort to rebuild her towns, almost at any cost. France, humiliated by defeat and enemy occupation and weakened by political division, was a slow starter, but before long she recovered her vitality and her strength of purpose, and was able to make good use of methods which had already been tried and proved effective before the war. Britain and Sweden, the one victorious and the other neutral, and both at first under Socialist governments, offer the clearest examples of central control in planning and administration. But all were aiming, not merely at catching up on demand by making up arrears in building, but at realizing a new and higher standard by programmes of development.

There is one point on which all countries agreed, namely that a determined effort must be made to bring general rent restriction to an end, though they did not all proceed with this at the same rate. The decisive step in British policy was taken in 1957. The Rent Act of that year lowered the maximum rateable value of houses subject to rent control, and thus released at once some 400,000 in England and Wales. And it provided for the decontrol of other dwellings when new tenancies were negotiated—the so-called 'creeping decontrol'—which caused the release of another 500,000 in the first two years.[11] The general effect was not as catastrophic as some people had feared, but neither did it do as much to encourage building houses to let to working-class families as some people had hoped. The Act contained some rather complicated clauses designed to protect the interests of both landlords and tenants. In certain circumstances, such as when repairs were carried out, landlords might raise their rents to a prescribed limit. And rules were laid down governing the conditions under which tenants could be given notice to quit. But these regulations have not been very well observed, partly because they were not properly understood, and partly because they were deliberately ignored. Two years after the Act was passed it was found that some 20% of the controlled houses were let at rents higher than those permitted by the law.[12] More scandalous, but fortunately less widespread, was the use made by some utterly unscrupulous landlords of various 'tough' methods, including physical violence, to drive out sitting tenants whom the law protected, in order to let rooms at higher rents, a practice which came to be known as 'Rachmanism' after its most notorious exponent.

Meanwhile the Rent Tribunals set up in 1946 to assess, on application from tenants, the rent of furnished rooms continued to function. Their task is a hard one, but their area of operation is relatively small, covering potentially only 2% of the total stock of dwellings, and actually far less. For they can act only when invited to do so, and many tenants who might get a reduction of rent are deterred by the thought of the ways in which their landlord might try to get his own back. The Tribunals can also extend security of tenure, and repeat the process, of families not otherwise protected, if they think the situation justifies this. They are interesting as an example of a form of rough social justice administered by laymen. They try to value premises in terms, not of market prices, but rather of the intrinsic character and condition of the rooms, and they must decide whether or not to extend security of tenure according to which course would cause the greater hardship. The first procedure is similar to that adopted by many local authorities in harmonizing the rents of old and new houses under their control, and the latter has long been followed by County Court Judges in much of their work.

Of more fundamental importance than rent control are the measures taken to increase and maintain the supply of new houses. And on this international comparison can be illuminating. The comparison can most usefully be based, not on a multitude of details, but on operational concepts. For social policy is built around the concepts in terms of which politicians, experts, and the public think about social problems.

The first point to notice is that British policy seems to revolve around the two contrasted 'operational concepts' of houses built by public authorities for letting and houses built by private enterprise for selling—or one might say of Council houses and non-Council houses. The political parties have clashed over the respective roles of these two types of dwellings in the national programme. The Labour Party favoured the former, while the Conservatives, when they succeeded them in power, were eager to encourage the latter. So between 1948 and 1952 nearly 90% of the new houses were publicly built, but between 1953 and 1959 less than 50%, and in 1960 only 40%.[13]

It follows that the methods used to sustain and promote these two categories of building, both of which are essential to the programme as a whole (in whatever proportions combined), are also sharply distinct. Local authorities are assisted by subsidies, that is to say, annual payments of a fixed sum in respect of each house, for a limited period, to help meet the charges on the capital borrowed to build the house. The Labour government gave a general subsidy on all domestic building, which was to be supplemented from the rates. The Conservatives in 1956 abolished the general subsidy and replaced it by subsidies for special purposes, such as slum clearance, redevelopment, New Towns, and homes for old people. But these 'special' purposes in practice cover a great number of cases. In 1961 the general subsidy was reintroduced, at a lower level, and for the first time preference was given to local authorities having the greatest financial need. Local authorities are now free to decide whether to supplement the subsidies from the rates, and also whether to charge 'differential' rents, that is to say, rents varied according to the economic circumstances of the tenants. But the dislike of these is deep and widespread, because they involve a means test; so they have not been generally adopted.

Private building received its greatest stimulus when it was relieved of the obligation, imposed on it by the Labour government immediately after the war, to obtain a licence for every house built. The removal of this restriction gave it the opportunity, but not the means, to forge ahead. Financially it is assisted by the 'negative subsidy' of remission of tax on the charges payable on capital invested in building. The sums which the Exchequer forgoes in this way are very large indeed. Some critics object that public money is being given to private individuals by this system of tax rebates. Its defenders reply that the society needs houses and the private builders are supplying a large proportion of them; also that the State is free to levy taxes where it chooses, and that there is a difference between not taking away somebody's money and giving him money taken from somebody else, which is what happens in the case of a 'positive subsidy'. One valid objection to the system is that it makes it very difficult to get a general view of what is happening, or to judge whether resources are going where they are most needed. Another, having considerable force, is that, since direct taxes are progressive, the largest benefit is reaped by the largest incomes.

The basic approach to housing policy in continental Europe is different, for it is not dominated by the two contrasted concepts of public and private building. To take their place policy has been trying to evolve and to render 'operational' the single concept of 'social housing'. This implies that the measures adopted by a government to ensure the production of houses for those whose needs are not met by the free market economy should be regarded as a special kind of social service, and that this applies to all such houses, whether produced by public, quasi-public, or even private agencies. The term appears in the first (1958) survey of the social situation in the Common Market countries, and by 1961 it had become a chapter heading.[14] Financial aid is given in all the usual forms, of subsidies, cheap or interest-free loans, tax rebates and so on, and embraces all houses in the 'social' category, though not necessarily in the same form or on the same terms. In the centre of the picture, filling the gap between the public and private categories, stand those housing societies, co-operatives and autonomous semi-public corporations which had already appeared before the Second World War, and have become far more conspicuous after it.

A few examples will help to explain the situation. In Sweden the execution of policy is directed by a government agency, the Royal Housing Board, which operates a system that lays down the terms on which all types of builder—public, co-operative, and private—can raise the capital to finance their enterprises. The proportion of the capital that must be provided by the builder from his own funds is 15% for private builders, 5% for co-operatives, and nothing for public authorities. The remainder is obtained partly on mortgage from commercial agencies, at controlled rates of interest (of which the Housing Board pays a proportion as a subsidy), and partly on loan from the Board itself. The co-operative housing societies are independent organizations, some of them started by occupational and trade groups, and they carry the principle of co-ownership and joint management right down to the level of the individual block of flats or housing scheme.[15]

France began by granting loans at 2% interest to Societies for building dwellings to be let to bombed-out families at rents below a fixed maximum. It went on to develop co-operative organizations of which the so-called HLM (Habitations à Louer Modéré) is the outstanding one. It is a successor to the pre-war HBM (Habitations à Bon Marché), and operates on a more generous definition of 'social housing' by accepting tenants with higher incomes. In status it falls between the governmental Royal Housing Board and the independent co-operatives of Sweden, being semi-official or quasi-public in character.[16] Another interesting feature of French housing is the 1% payroll levy on industry used for building homes for workers. The Italian equivalent to the French HLM is the INA-Casa (National Insurance Institute—Housing), which is financed by a payroll tax and a government subsidy, and is therefore a degree more official.[17]

Germany is a rather different story. It had, like the other countries, a system of subsidies and cheap loans for 'social housing', but it went much further in the encouragement of private building by tax privileges of so extensive and complex a kind that they were open to serious abuse. Owing to the scandals caused by this, the privileges had to be modified and, in some cases, dropped. The net result, however, was a volume of building unequalled elsewhere, but at a cost that cannot be exactly estimated, because the effort was stimulated by tax concessions more than by loans or subsidies.[18]

There is contained within these policies a common element which is the idea of using financial devices to underpin, as it were, the market in 'social housing', and then to let it function as nearly as possible as a normal free market would. The German version of this idea is contained in Dr Erhard's so-called 'social market economy', which claims to give freedom to the competitive market under conditions that guarantee social welfare—a sort of competitive Welfare State. German economists differ as to whether this doctrine has any precise meaning, but in the case of housing it clearly implies the use of rent allowances rather than rent restriction. It was embodied in the 'social rent and housing law' of 1960, which aimed at terminating both rent control and the allocation of dwellings by the Housing Offices.[19] All this is in sharp contrast with the British practice of keeping public housing out of the market and administering it directly and in detail by the local authorities and their officers.

But the latest move in British policy has done something to modify the contrast by placing a new emphasis on the part that can be played by Housing Societies. Housing trusts and associations had, of course, existed in England since the latter part of the nineteenth century as private, voluntary organizations to build homes for certain classes of persons in certain areas. Some, like the Peabody fund, were charitable (though paying a limited dividend on the capital invested), and others were co-operative. The Housing Act of 1936 had given them a legal status within the category of Friendly Societies, and they were allowed to borrow from the Public Works Loan Board on the same terms as local authorities, but only up to 90% of the capital required in each case. After the war scant attention was paid to their interests, and they were treated in general in the same way as other private enterprises at a time when public enterprise was being given effective priority. Beveridge, writing in 1948, said of them that 'housing societies today, from the Government of the day, get warm words and cold comfort'.[20]

The situation remained virtually unchanged until 1961, when a Housing Act authorized the advancement of direct loans to Housing

Associations up to a total of £25 million to help schemes approved by the Minister. This modest step was followed by a somewhat bolder scheme outlined in a White Paper in 1963 and incorporated in a Bill in the following year. This has interesting features. First, it has the explicit aim of encouraging the formation of a network of non-profit-making Housing Societies to 'provide and manage rented houses, or houses on a co-ownership basis'. No such initiative had been taken hitherto. Secondly there is to be a Housing Corporation established by Parliament and subject to general directives issued by the Minister, but in other respects autonomous. It is not to be 'the servant or agent of the Crown' nor to have any of the immunities or privileges which that status would carry. The Corporation will be provided with capital, up to a maximum of fifty or, if the Minister decides, a hundred million pounds, to lend to independent Societies. Thirdly, the whole scheme is to operate as a joint one in which the Corporation and the private Building Societies (which are at present the chief source of loans on mortgage to private builders or purchasers of houses) will function as partners, under regulations to be included in the Act. The idea is that the Building Societies should advance about two-thirds and the Corporation one-third of the capital for each scheme.

There are some resemblances between this project and the systems found in continental Europe, but they are superficial. For, although private enterprise is to be encouraged, by the grant of financial facilities, to co-operate with a public corporation under regulations issued by the government, the dichotomy between the public and private sectors will remain. Nothing could be stronger than the insistence, in the Bill, that the Corporation is not an agent of the Crown; and it will lend only to private builders, the local authorities continuing to raise their capital from a different source. Nor is there any suggestion that the Societies helped by the Corporation are to confine themselves to 'social housing', or to houses let at limited rents to families of limited means. This concept, so far as it can be said to exist, will still apply only to Council houses. Nevertheless, if the effect were to bring into being a substantial volume of building within the private sector that is definitely non-commercial, that would undoubtedly weaken the force of the dichotomy and perhaps lead towards a more integrated housing policy.

Another significant feature of European policy is that integration is found, not only within housing policy itself, but also between housing policy and social security. The payroll levies in France and

Italy are at least very similar in character to the percentage on wages paid as a contribution to social insurance. They imply that housing is, in some measure, a social service. Then it is common practice for social insurance funds to be used in part for 'social housing'. Pension funds may be invested in homes for old people, and in Germany the Youth Programme includes money for improving the homes of the young. Thirdly, to quote the European Economic Community's survey for 1961, there has been a general trend to 'substitute aid to persons for aid to bricks'. In France this has taken the form of a rent allowance to insured persons based on the relation between the family income and the rent of the home. This, said the Survey, 'could be called, if it came to be extensively applied, "social security in housing" '.[21] In Sweden, as of 1960, rent allowances are paid direct to the landlord in respect of families with incomes below a certain level, and taking account of the number of dependent children, provided the house comes up to the required standard.[22]

British policy for the first decade after the war was thus dominated by rent restriction and housing subsidies. Both led to anomalies which legislation from 1957 onwards has been trying to eradicate. The trouble was deep-seated. For both these devices operated without reference to individual needs, just as compulsory social insurance operated in terms of averages. But, unlike social insurance on the Beveridge plan, they were applied only to a section of the society, and that almost a fortuitous one. The line dividing restricted from unrestricted houses, on the basis of their value, could not be regarded as a true 'poverty line' for the families that lived in them. Council tenants were, it is true, carefully selected. But in the first place the priorities that had to be given to those evicted by redevelopment plans, to those needing special types of accommodation and, above all, to those who had been resident in the area for several years, meant that many whose need for a house was genuine and urgent stood little chance of getting one for a very long time. In the second place the benefits accorded to the fortunate ones were ultimately financial—they got a subsidized house for less than its true value; but the tests on which priorities of claim were determined were 'welfare' tests. They related to overcrowding, size of family, state of health, and so on. Claimants were given a place in the queue because they were living in intolerable conditions rather than because they were abnormally poor. So, when things settled down, it was found that many tenants enjoyed low rents subsidized out of rates and taxes paid in part by people worse off than themselves.

Finally, local authorities have a dual role to play. They are responsible in a general way for the whole physical environment, and they are responsible in a particular way for the houses built or controlled by them. In their first capacity they can plan, but they have no initiative in executing the plan, except for the general lay-out and the public buildings. In their second capacity they initiate, execute, and administer their estates, as builders and landlords. The harmonious combination of these two functions is not always easy. The troubles that British housing policy has encountered may be due (to quote two recent authorities) to the difficulty of maintaining a large programme of publicly owned housing and at the same time encouraging private investment in new housing, and to the 'curious British system' by which subsidies 'are given for houses rather than for families'.[23]

1 White Paper on Housing, May 1963, p. 2
2 Stanley Alderson, *Britain in the Sixties—Housing*, p. 59
3 M. Young and P. Willmott, *Family and Kinship in East London*, p. 155
4 J. B. Cullingworth, 'Social Implications of Overspill' in *Sociological Review*, 1960, pp. 92–3
5 H. M. Wright, quoted in J. B. Cullingworth, *Housing Needs and Planning Policy*, p. 145
6 A. Sauvy, 'The Housing Problem in France' in *International Labour Review*, 1947, vol. 55, p. 237
7 D. V. Donnison, Christine Cockburn and T. Corlett, *Housing since the Rent Act*, p. 19
8 Mark Abrams, *The Condition of the British People*, p. 84; Ministry of Labour Family Expenditure Survey
9 Paul F. Wendt, *Housing Policy, the Search for Solutions*, p. 75
10 White Paper on Housing, 1963, p. 7
11 Donnison et al., op. cit., pp. 30–2
12 ibid., p. 38
13 Wendt, op. cit., pp. 50–1; White Paper on Housing, February 1961
14 *Exposé sur la situation sociale dans la Communauté*, for 1958, p. 100, and for 1961, p. 203
15 Wendt, op. cit., pp. 67–80; unpublished report by Mrs Christine Cockburn
16 *Exposé . . .* , for 1959, p. 259, and for 1961, pp. 214–16
17 *Exposé . . .* , for 1958, p. 99

18   Wendt, op. cit., pp. 124–44
19   *Exposé* . . . , for 1960, p. 191, and for 1961, p. 210–11; Article on
     'Soziale Markwirtschaft' in *Handwörterbuch der Sozialwissenschaften*,
     1956, vol. 9
20   Lord Beveridge, Voluntary Action, p. 106 n
21   *Exposé* . . . , for 1961, p. 205, and for 1959, p. 271
22   *Social Benefits in Sweden*, p. 15
23   Wendt, op. cit., p. 271; J. B. Cullingworth, *Housing in Transition*,
     p. 223

12

Executants of social policy

'Social Policy' has been taken in this book to refer to the policy of governments, and no attempt has been made to survey the independent activities of private organizations. But the question of the location of the frontier between the two arose at an early stage, in the arguments between the Majority and the Minority of the Royal Commission on the Poor Law, and has cropped up from time to time since then. It is the purpose of this chapter to supplement the few remarks already made on this subject, and in doing so to take a look at the role of the professional social worker.

When the publicly administered Poor Law was set up to take over a part of what had till then been the province of private, communal, or ecclesiastical charity, the location of the frontier was easy to see. The public service was for paupers, the private for the deserving poor; the public was deterrent, the private benevolent; the public was limited to what the law prescribed, the private could range as widely as it pleased—to explore dark corners of social distress that might otherwise pass unnoticed, and to devise and put to the test new forms of relief and remedy. Then came the great age of the pioneers, prominent among whom were many famous women like Elizabeth Fry, Florence Nightingale, Josephine Butler, or Octavia Hill. For the door that voluntary social service opened to innovation was one through which women could enter public life, in a sphere not already reserved for men. It is said that when, in 1818, Elizabeth Fry was invited to give evidence to a Committee of the House of Commons on the state of the prisons, she was 'the first woman other than a queen to be called into the councils of the Government in an official manner to advise on matters of public concern'.[1]

By the middle of the nineteenth century voluntary action presented a somewhat disorderly picture. The work of the pioneers was, for the most part, practical and disciplined, and inspired by a clear purpose. It produced results of lasting value. But there were also a multitude of charitable bequests, many of which served no useful purpose and many societies whose bounty, distributed with too little discrimination, often missed its true mark. Charity was sadly disorganized, or so it seemed to those who, in 1869, founded the Charity Organization Society. It is difficult today to assess fairly the work of the COS and of C. S. Loch, the man who directed its affairs for thirty-eight years. Its philosophy is repugnant to the modern mind and, as we saw, was condemned both from inside (by Canon Barnett) and from outside its ranks (by Beatrice Webb) while it was still in its prime. And yet, while it was reactionary on some points (such as old-age pensions), it was a pioneer on others (such as the treatment of mentally afflicted, and the employment of hospital almoners); and it did much to develop the methods still used today by social case-work agencies.

Its contribution to case-work methods was directly derived from its philosophy, that is to say, from the better elements in it, which were more clearly expressed in the teaching of Loch himself than they were manifested in the behaviour of some of his disciples. His aim was to abolish pauperism, not merely to relieve it. 'Pauperism', he wrote, 'is the social enemy of the modern State. The State wants citizens.' In pursuit of this goal 'private service in a great measure takes the place of private relief'. And all that is done must be based on the fullest possible knowledge of the circumstances of the case. Charity 'requires a social discipline; it works through sympathy; it depends on science. Its first thought is to understand, and to treat with the reverence that comes from understanding' the individual, the family and the community. And the treatment must be 'adequate' to effect a cure, and to restore the recipient to a state of self-sufficiency.

There is little to quarrel with here. The theme is sound, but there were some unpleasant overtones. 'Adequate help' was considered to be possible only for those with the will to help themselves, and these were the 'deserving' cases. The rest were to be left to the Poor Law. They were at first referred to in the records as the 'undeserving', but later as those 'unlikely to benefit'. This category included, not only the drunken, the immoral, and the lazy, but also those afflicted with a misfortune, physical, mental, or social, which the services of the COS were not competent to cure. Secondly, 'private service' was also referred to as 'personal influence', which meant the influence exerted by the superior moral character and social wisdom of the social workers and committee members. And thirdly, it was assumed that the roots of distress were to be found in the individual and his personal history, not in the social order which, as regards its basic class structure, must be accepted.[2] There is a good deal to quarrel with here, and yet it was precisely this preoccupation with the individual case, and this search for a full understanding and effective treatment of it, that enabled the COS to construct, out of elements many of which were already current somewhere, an integrated system of social case-work.

Very briefly this system included, first and foremost, enquiry, by questioning the applicant and visiting the home. From the enquiry were compiled the case-papers, and the report and recommendations. These were submitted to the Committee, which alone could decide the action to be taken. For the Committee, composed of 'gentry', was the policy-maker, and the social workers were its servants. These were in part volunteers and in part salaried, but all must be trained. The Committee must realize, they were told, that 'the difficult and troublesome task of Training Volunteer Workers . . . is one of their chief and most important duties'. This was an innovation and, in due course, the COS promoted the foundation of a School of Sociology, under E. J. Urwick, to put it into effect. This School subsequently (in 1912) passed into the hands of the London School of Economics, much to the distress of its original promoters who feared that it would not receive there the firm ethical guidance that it needed.[3] Finally, the general setting of this system of social case-work was to be a network of District Committees which would co-ordinate the work of all the voluntary agencies in the area, and maintain the closest possible relations with the local public authorities.

It was along these lines that the COS operated in London, under the patronage of some of the highest personages in the land. It was not an isolated force, but was moving with the stream that was flowing at the same time through other channels in Britain, on the Continent, and in the United States. The net effect of all these developments was to bring the voluntary and statutory agencies closer together. The ideas launched by the pioneers and their societies became the common property of both, as did the modernized, twentieth-century versions of the methods of social work and the training of social workers. And the voluntary bodies, with their up-to-date and efficient administration and their large, national federations, came to look, and to act, more like a public service. The way was open for the partnership of the inter-war years. This was a partnership in which the two sides met well-nigh on equal terms. The principles and practice by which they worked had been shaped more by private than by public influences, and the prestige of the voluntary organizations stood high. Meanwhile the public services, though still restricted in scope by modern standards, were growing in range and strength and in a sense of sovereign responsibility. The war and the social policy of the post-war years speeded this growth, and the partnership, too, was yet more firmly cemented, but the statutory authorities were now indisputably the senior partner. So much so that some people thought the voluntary societies had had their day, and would now decline into comparative insignificance. This has not happened. They have, on the whole, managed to serve the purposes of public policy (which are also their own), and to accept financial help, and sometimes instructions, from the public authorities, while preserving the spirit of independence and the freedom of thought and of speech without which voluntary action must lose its savour.

The dominant position of the State expresses itself in various ways, but is based on its undisputed, ultimate, overall responsibility for social welfare. This has led it in some cases to take the initiative in the establishment of a voluntary organization to meet a need of which it has become conscious. A peculiar example of this is the foundation by the government in 1938, in anticipation of a possible war, of the Women's Voluntary Service (WVS) staffed by voluntary workers, led by a Chairman nominated by the government, and financed from public funds. It took instructions from above and, as Beveridge said, 'it has held itself ready to do anything that it was asked to do, has become auxiliary to more than twenty government departments and has co-operated with local authorities in more than 100 different operations'.[4] And yet, in spite of all this official control, it preserved the spirit of a voluntary organization, and it had (and still has) only an absolute minimum of paid staff.

Very different is the case of the Central Association for the Care of the Mentally Defective, created in 1913 on the suggestion of the Chairman of the Board of Control. Its function was to stimulate and co-ordinate the work of voluntary societies in this field, and to provide an organization to which both voluntary and statutory bodies could be affiliated. The same model was adopted by the Central Council for Infant and Child Welfare in 1919. These were not quasi-voluntary bodies set up to do the bidding of public authorities, but fully independent societies with a policy and a programme of their own. The Board of Control pointed out, with reference to the first of them, not only that voluntary bodies could render services lying outside the competence of the public authorities 'in the present state of the law', but also that they could engage in publicity and influence public opinion in a way that would be improper for a public authority—a rather remarkable position to take up, in view of the mixed constitution of the body concerned.[5]

Sometimes the process was reversed; the initiative came from the voluntary organization and public authority took over the service, or drew it into its ambit, later. In the case of services for the evacuated and homeless during the war, for instance, 'it was the voluntary organizations', says Professor Titmuss, 'the Charity Organization Society, the Society of Friends, the Settlement workers, the London Council of Social Service and many others—who helped to hold the line during this period while the official machine was beginning to take effective action', but the 'official machine' assumed control in due course.[6] Or take the Citizens' Advice Bureaux. These were invented before the war by the National Council of Social Service, and developed into a general service run by voluntary bodies to help the private citizen to understand the nature and extent of his public rights and duties, and to take full advantage of the public, as well as the voluntary, services. As the war drew to a close, the government dropped broad hints to the effect that in future they and the local authorities would do most of their own information work. 'I do feel,' said the Minister of Health in 1945, 'that the Citizens' Advice Bureaux would be wise to accept the principle that both Government Departments and local authorities must make their services known to the people and must not rely on others to do it.' And a similar, but yet blunter, remark by the Parliamentary Secretary to the Ministry of Labour provoked the comment that what he was saying was, 'You have done a wonderful job; we are going to pinch it.'[7] But though many of these Bureaux were closed and some were replaced by information offices run as a public service, the movement survived and in recent years there has been a strong swing back in favour of the voluntary system.

If one tried to classify the forms of co-operation between voluntary and statutory agencies at the local level, the catalogue would run something like this: the voluntary body is expressly entrusted with the performance of tasks on behalf of the local authority at the expense of the latter (the so-called 'agency' schemes); the voluntary body works closely with the statutory and is subsidized; the voluntary body acts independently but nevertheless receives a subvention from public funds; the voluntary body works in close accord with the local authority but receives no subvention. Cases of the first type were noted in earlier chapters; this kind of co-operation is almost universal in services for the deaf and dumb, is common in those for other handicapped persons, and has been the accepted practice in the provision of meals for old people by the WVS. Examples of the second type are legion. We will give just one, by way of illustration, from a survey of social work in a small county borough. The Moral Welfare Association appoints the social worker who looks after the unmarried mothers, and four-fifths of her salary is paid by the local authority. She has two committees, one of voluntary workers and the local clergy, and one semi-official which meets in the office of the Medical Officer of Health who takes the minutes and reports to the Health Committee.[8] A good example of a voluntary service which pursues its own, independent course, but nevertheless receives some support from public funds, is marriage guidance. The activities of the National Marriage Guidance Council, though raising delicate issues, enjoy enough general approval to warrant this financial support. The societies which do not get grants, and which are careful to point out the fact in their appeals (suggesting thereby that it is exceptional), include both some that are experimental or highly specialized or operating on quite a small scale, some that are too controversial in character, like the Family Planning Association, and, of course, others which seem able to manage on their own resources.

It is significant that the public money contributed to voluntary societies is not voted as a block grant, given because of some general idea that voluntary enterprise deserves public support. It appears on the budgets of the appropriate central or local departments as aid to organizations working in their field, and is thus a direct expression of the partnership between the two types of agency. As the National Council of Social Service says in its handbook on Voluntary Social Services, 'the contributions are a recognition of the work done by the voluntary organization in a social service in which the statutory authority is interested'.[9]

The opportunity for voluntary organizations to continue to function today, in spite of the expansion of the public services, arises partly from the positive assets they have to offer and partly from the limitations that restrict the work of the statutory authorities. The most obvious of the latter is the sheer lack of resources. For, as the National Council of Social Service says, with reference to help for the handicapped, 'finance and shortage of trained staff set a limit to what a local authority can do, whatever its policy'.[10] But, as we have seen, a limit may also be set by the fact that legislation has not yet conferred the necessary powers (though likely to do so soon), or that, although permissive legislation has authorized a particular service, local opinion is not yet ready to embark on it, or that certain services involve social or religious attitudes not shared by all. Another factor which can check the action of a public authority is that it may feel that it should not offer a particular service unless it can be made available to all who need it; and that may well be impossible for the time being. But a voluntary organization can, and often does, select its clients to suit its means, as did the Family Service Units when they embarked on their work with problem families.

Among the positive assets of voluntary social service are ideas, of which, although it would not now claim to have a monopoly, it is still a very fruitful source; and a freedom to test them experimentally, which is still somewhat greater than that enjoyed by the public authorities. Then there are the obvious assets of money and men—or more particularly women—to add to the supply of these indispensable commodities in public hands. The money still flows in, but through rather different channels than before. Less of it comes from the 'great patrons', and more proportionately from Charitable Trusts, from business and industry, from a multitude of small subscribers, and from the proceeds of appeals, flag days, and the sale of Christmas cards. The personnel cannot be regarded as a net gain to social service, for much of it consists of salaried workers who could equally well be employed by public authorities. But many who can offer only part of their time, or who are by temperament averse to becoming civil servants, would not otherwise be available.

Finally there is that elusive thing, the spirit of voluntary action. We think of it, ideally, as combining devoted service, freshness of mind, and moral energy. Undoubtedly it exists, but does it count for much in a modern voluntary organization, which is, in form, a bureaucracy administering a professional staff? It is futile to speculate on this question, but it is worth while to remember, if we are comparing the voluntary with the public agencies, that the people who man the Committees which run the former and the local Councils that direct the latter are today very much the same, or at least are people of the same kind, inspired by the same motives. The significant difference between them is that which relates to the nature of their responsibility.

Voluntary action, said Beveridge, has been based on one or other of two principles, philanthropy and mutual aid.[11] In a philanthropic society the givers are sharply distinct from the receivers of charitable aid and are responsible, not to them, but only to their conscience. In a mutual aid society, givers and receivers are the same, and the managers are responsible to the members. The public services in the modern democratic 'Welfare State', or, as Beveridge preferred to call it, 'Welfare Society', in which all citizens are potentially both givers and receivers, are administered by people who are, constitutionally, the servants of those they serve, and responsible to them. Representative democracy has taken on the character of a mutual aid society. But voluntary organizations cannot adopt the principles of either democracy or mutual aid, unless they have a stable constituency to which their management can be responsible, which is the case only with those of the Friendly Society type, and perhaps with Community Centres based on the neighbourhood, and with some societies for the permanently blind or deaf. For the rest the principle remains that of philanthropy, and the question is, to what can philanthropy be held responsible, other than its own conscience?

There are two possible answers. First there is the vicarious responsibility to the electorate that comes from close co-operation with the public authorities in implementing a social policy that has been democratically determined. Secondly there is the responsibility of a profession to its clients. There is no agreed definition of a 'profession', but one may assume that its two chief attributes are the possession of particular skills and knowledge usually acquired by training and tested by examination, and a relationship of mutual trust between the professional man and his client, based on the qualifications of the former and his code of professional conduct. Is social work a profession in this sense? This is a controversial issue which concerns the statutory agencies even more than the voluntary, because they employ more 'career' social workers and have more to do with their 'professional' associations. These are anxious to defend the professional status of their members, but some of their claims have been criticized as being extravagant. 'The pretence that professional case-work is of a piece with other more established professions', writes Baroness Wootton, 'can only be maintained by disregarding some very obvious differences.' Her complaint is that social workers, eager to be ranked on a level with the higher professions, lay claim to knowledge and skills which they do not really possess. If, she continues, they were content to restrict their activities to what is practicable, they would not lose by this. For in such circumstances 'a genuine professional status as well as a genuine parallel with other professions becomes actually easier to achieve'.[12]

In exploring this parallel we may start by noting that undoubtedly forms of training for social work have existed for a long time, but very many practising social workers have never been trained. This, however, used to be true, but has steadily become less so, of the teaching profession. More important is the fact that there is no clearly marked point, or level, at which the training leads to a universally recognized professional qualification. It is generally agreed among those responsible for them that the university courses leading to Diplomas or Degrees in Social Studies (or Social Science) do not constitute professional training, but only a basic preparation for it. They should be followed by one of the specialized courses in mental health or child care and so forth, or the more recently established courses in 'generic case-work'. But many social workers terminate their training at the 'social studies' level and are accepted by employers as professionally qualified. The Younghusband Working Party (referred to in Chapter 9) deplored this situation and proposed to remedy it by instituting, outside the universities, courses to which the 'integration of theory and practice' would give a more genuine vocational character. They should be nationally organized and lead to the granting of a National Certificate in Social Work. This recommendation has been adopted. But the Working Party did not claim that the Certificate should rank as a professional qualification. It spoke of those obtaining it as 'officers with general training in social work', reserving the term 'professional' for those who have taken the advanced university courses. But, if social work is to rank as a profession, it must include those who have taken the Younghusband Courses, which are certainly comparable with those taken by teachers and others of the 'lesser' professions.

Turning briefly to some other aspects of professionalism, we may feel that the relationship of trust between social worker and client is not always of such profound consequence as in the case of the doctor or the solicitor, but without it social work of many kinds could not go on. And finally it is true that the professional associations of social workers are concerned not only with conditions of work, but also with principles of conduct. So we may at least say, adapting a phrase used by Carr-Saunders and Wilson of the nurses, that the vocation of social work is becoming professionalized.[13] And there is a strong case for urging that the process should continue.

It is important, however, that social workers should not, in their eagerness for professional status, claim to possess and attempt to practise skills which they do not really possess. And Baroness Wootton's chief complaint is that this is precisely what they are doing, especially in the United States. There is some truth in the charge. The social worker of Victorian days was a moral preceptor; her successor today, it is alleged, aspires to be a psychological 'counsellor', and she is not qualified for this role. But there is no need, on this account, to reduce her to the position of a sort of superior daily help *cum* contact-woman. The social worker's task cannot be limited to the satisfaction of material and physical needs, because the capacity to make use of help depends very much on how the help is offered. And in many of the cases with which social work deals the material factor may be the beginning of the trouble, but it is not the end of it. On the other hand the social worker must not pretend that she has the skill to diagnose and treat psychological ailments or the authority to tell her fellow-citizens how they should live their lives. But between these extremes there lies an area in which both material help and personal support and advice can be given by those qualified to do so in part by training, in part by experience, and in part also by acceptance of a code of professional conduct. And it is not foolish to imagine that a voluntary organization may find that the responsibility of a profession to its clients can in some measure take the place of the responsibility of a Friendly Society to its members or of a democracy to its citizens.

1 Janet Whitney, *Elizabeth Fry, Quaker Heroine*, quoted in Lord Beveridge, *Voluntary Action*, p. 126
2 C. S. Loch, *How to Help Cases of Distress*, 1895, and *Charity Organization*, 1905, *passim*; C. L. Mowat, *The Charity Organization Society 1869–1913*, pp. 36–7 and 71
3 Mowat, op. cit., pp. 107 and 112

4 Beveridge, op. cit., p. 137

5 Madeline Rooff, *Voluntary Societies and Social Policy*, pp. 58, 105, and 143–4

6 R. M. Titmuss, *Problems of Social Policy*, pp. 261–2

7 National Council of Social Service, Report of National Conference, May 1945, on 'Citizens' Advice Bureaux after the War', pp. 4 and 8

8 Barbara N. Rodgers and Julia Dixon, *Portrait of Social Work*, pp. 126 and 140

9 National Council of Social Service, *Handbook and Directory of Voluntary Social Services*, 1960, p. 13

10 National Council of Social Service, *Help for the Handicapped*, p. 62

11 Beveridge, op. cit., p. 8

12 Barbara Wootton, *Social Science and Social Pathology*, pp. 287 and 296

13 A. M. Carr-Saunders and P. A. Wilson, *The Professions*, p. 121

13

Retrospect and prospect

Looking back over the past sixty or seventy years one can see the salient features of the story of social policy standing out in strong relief. Having once been confined to the helpless and hopeless on the fringe of the community, it has come to include the whole population. Voluntary action has expanded and organized itself on a model that differs little in function and method from the public services. And the economy, out of the proceeds of its growing productivity, now offers, as part of the earnings of labour, benefits which were formerly provided only by schemes run by the State. Consequently there have taken place at many points a convergence of principles and an integration of practices which together account for the present pattern of social policy and for the problems that still remain unsolved.

There was first the integration of the apparatus of social security itself. It took the form of a bold 'pooling of risks', and of the amalgamation of the previously separate insurance schemes into a consolidated whole. But, although fidelity to the classic principles of insurance has been abandoned, something of the legacy of the insurance approach still remains. In most countries the conditions under which, and the machinery through which, a benefit is paid depend, in some cases at least, on the cause of the loss of income— whether old age, sickness, unemployment, industrial accident, widowhood, or anything else. A striking example of this is the aid given to fatherless families in Britain. For, as Margaret Wynn points out, the benefit received in respect of the child depends on the status of the mother (widowed, divorced, or deserted) and of the child (legitimate or illegitimate), and, if the father is dead, on whether he died of an illness, was killed in an industrial accident, or fell in battle.[1] Yet the need to be met is the same in all cases.

Insurance and assistance, too, have everywhere experienced not

integration, perhaps, but assimilation. This was observed in the
United States in the 1940's where, it was said, 'social insurance and
social assistance are approaching one another from opposite
starting points, each assuming features proper to the other until
they meet, as it were, in the centre and merge'.[2] But the merger
cannot be complete, since the claim to assistance must, in the nature
of things, begin with a statement of means, but the claim to insurance benefit does not. Nor have we yet got that 'unification of
social insurance and assistance in respect of administration' advocated in the Beveridge Report.[3]

In the case of services, as distinct from cash benefits, there have
been two trends. First, the growth of a close partnership between
the statutory and voluntary agencies, and secondly, the movement
to rectify excessive specialization in the welfare services. This has
caused more weight to be given to the common element in both
the needs of those served and the qualities required in those who
serve them; hence the interest in the idea of a 'general purpose
social worker', and the proposal, coming from several directions
at once, that local authorities should have at their disposal a
general family case-work service.

Next comes the question of harmonizing what is publicly provided with the similar schemes run by private firms. Sick-pay can
be obtained from both, and so can pensions; the State looks after
the unemployed, while industry does what it can (or thinks it can)
for the 'redundant'. But the benefits offered by the State are universal and standardized, while those offered by commerce and industry
are not. Pensions, as we have seen, present the greatest problem.
The State cannot leave private enterprise in sole occupation of the
field, but a State monopoly of pensions deprives employers of control over what can be an important factor in labour recruitment
and labour relations. Some countries have created such a monopoly,
or something very near to it. The present British scheme is a compromise which is generally held to be unsatisfactory, but there is as
yet no certainty what will take its place.

Then there is the integration of social policy with economic
policy. Everybody agrees that this must take place, but opinions
differ as to the lines along which the process should go forward.
Beveridge insisted that social security was possible only in con-
junction with a policy of full employment. Housing necessarily
involves a programme consistent with the present and the expected
state of the economy. Social security funds may be used to finance

quasi-public enterprise, but their accumulation, if carried too far, can upset the capital market. Wage-related social security schemes, and the substitution of modern superannuation for old-style pensions, represent an assimilation of a social service to the practices and the value system of the economy. The benefits become part of the total remuneration of work and are governed by the same principles as other earnings. Even Socialists can accept this, provided the system of earnings to which the benefits are assimilated is itself acceptable.

But the most important question that arises in this context is 'how much does our social policy cost, and how much can the economy afford?' Economists who specialize in this field tell us that the percentage of the Gross National Product devoted to social services rose from 2·6 in 1900 to 11·3 in 1938 and to 18·0 in 1950, and it was 17·8 in 1961.[4] But these figures include expenditure on education and food subsidies, two large items not treated in this book. They do, however, help us to see things in perspective. The big rise in the percentage figure before the Second World War, when there were still no food subsidies, makes the increase since then look much less spectacular. The ILO figures for 1957, giving public and quasi-public expenditure on insurance, assistance, health and family allowances as a percentage of National Income, were 12·1 for the United Kingdom, 18·9 for France, 20·8 for Germany, and 6·0 for the United States. They were offered with a warning that exact comparison is not possible.[5]

The contrast between Germany and the United States reminds us that the question 'what can the economy afford?' must be taken to refer to total, and not only to public expenditure. The burden on the economy is not lightened by transferring expenditure from public to private funds, any more than it is increased when people are made to pay for medical care through taxes instead of by fees. But the growth in public provision is not due mainly to transfers of this kind, but to a net increase in the sum of resources of all kinds devoted to the social services. The economic effect of this depends on the other uses to which these resources might have been put, and their relative scarcity is therefore an important consideration. Now, although the social services employ some people possessed of scarce abilities, like those that go to make a good doctor or surgeon, they do not make heavy demands on the principal skills used in modern industry nor do they use much expensive and complicated machinery. They employ a lot of part-time labour,

some of it voluntary, and a good many women who might otherwise not enter the labour market at all. So taking it 'weight for
weight' as it were, the demands of the social services on the economy
are comparatively modest.

It is often said that cash benefits, as distinct from services, involve no more than a redistribution of income, or purchasing-
power, which imposes no extra burden on the economy. So the
question we should ask is not whether we can afford them, but
whether we want them. This is clearly true when they are financed
from general taxation; the money is gathered in by one administrative apparatus and paid out again by another. But even so, taxes
can have a depressing effect on the economy, even when most of
the money collected flows back—by and large and in the long run—
to the people from whom it was taken. And that is roughly what
happens when the entire population is included in the scheme.

But, as we have seen, there is a growing tendency to raise the
money, or a large part of it, by means of a graduated payroll tax,
which becomes an item in the labour costs of production. A portion
of it, but only a portion, may well be covered by a reduction in the
current earnings of labour, or a postponement of an increase in
those earnings which would otherwise have taken place. It is
possible, that is to say, that wages would have been a bit higher if
employers did not have to pay contributions into an insurance
fund; but they might also have been a bit lower if contributions
were not deducted from the employees' pay-packet. But it is natural
and proper that the introduction, or the improvement, of benefits
of this kind should increase labour costs, because these measures
are part of a social policy for raising the standard of living. The
conclusion—in simplified form—is that a self-financed superannuation scheme (like the Swedish graduated pensions) can be
introduced without trouble only when conditions are such that the
economy can absorb an increase in the labour costs of production;
but, once safely introduced, its continued operation presents no
special problems. It is simply a different way of paying an economic
wage. Finally there is the question of the integration of the Welfare
State with the Affluent Society, taking each as the expression of a
political philosophy. It is too early to offer a final judgement, but
the evidence suggests that intregration of a kind is gradually taking
place. Less is heard in the middle sixties of the more extreme views
expressed in the middle fifties—such as that social insurance should
be abolished and replaced by a limited system of social assistance,

that freedom should be given to 'opt out' of the National Health Service, or that people should be given 'vouchers' with which to buy places in private schools instead of being offered free places in public ones.

The critics of the welfare philosophy of fair shares and mutual aid argued that economic individualism was the proper philosophy of affluence because there was enough for everybody, and the few who failed to get their share could, and would, be assisted. But it is now clear that this was an over-optimistic view of the state of the modern world. When the President of the United States, the prototype of the Affluent Society, thinks it appropriate to make the war against poverty a principal plank in his political platform it is obvious that the affluence that undoubtedly exists in greater measure than ever before does not make national concern with welfare obsolete. In such circumstances one cannot subscribe to the doctrine of an American writer on social work who has declared that 'welfare programs are, on the one hand, a Christian expression of compassion for our fellow men, and on the other hand insurance for the continued operation of the profit motive'.[6] Welfare programmes must, on the contrary, be regarded as one of the means by which affluence may be converted into both common and individual enjoyment. A realistic appraisal of welfare in terms of a civilized way of life is the natural antithesis of the crude acquisitiveness which many observers noted as a disquieting phenomenon in the 1950's. And an affluent society that embodied in itself this concept of welfare would be very different from the acquisitive society which Dr Zweig, looking at the events of that decade, thought had 'succeeded in expanding its frontiers and converting its natural antagonists to its own creed' by infecting the working classes.[7] We need not be so pessimistic as to believe that only a world war can induce society to progress in that direction.

The critics of the Welfare State also accused it of pursuing egalitarianism as an end in itself and of using social policy as an instrument for changing the structure of society. This might perhaps pass as a fair description of social policy in the first half of this century, but is not true of social policy today. For in the first place the typically modern form of social security is one in which individualism and mutual aid are harmoniously combined and incorporated in graduated schemes which are a collective way of allotting benefits on individual claims. They are not egalitarian. It is true that there is built into them some redistribution of income from the richer to the poorer, but this is of a controlled and limited amount, designed to narrow the gaps between the lowest layers of the economic pyramid, not to change its structure. Secondly, there is some truth in the assertion that the main effect of the Welfare State has been 'to provide free social services to the middle classes'.[8] This is inevitable when services previously confined to the lower income-groups are extended to the whole population. And even though one may prefer to say that the 'main effect' has been the raising of the general standard of the services, this can hardly be called egalitarianism for its own sake. Thirdly, no great effort is being made to reduce the range of income difference at the peak of the pyramid, or to curb the forces which, some people think, are tending to increase that range. Salaries become steadily more astronomical and the heavy burden of taxation imposed on them continues to be lightened by various tax concessions, while the great advantages that flow from the possession of capital are ever more ingeniously exploited. On this point there has not been a recon- ciliation of the two philosophies. Nevertheless the concept of an 'incomes policy' has entered the world of politics, and although none has yet been discovered that is acceptable to all parties, we may be approaching a situation in which incomes must not deviate too far from what such a policy would prescribe, if it existed, or the government would just *have* to introduce one.

It is easy, when studying social policy, to exaggerate its effects on society, both material and psychological. And this is especially the case now, when little room remains for any major new develop- ments. The structure of society, and the pattern of economic in- equality, depend primarily on the structure of the economy and the pattern of its rewards. It is only in education that social reforms alone could produce changes of any real magnitude. It has some- times been said that the benefits conferred by the social services sap the morale of the population. But full employment, high wages, easy profits, and reliance on powerful organizations have a greater influence on the will to work than the fact that schools and hospitals charge no fees.

All this does not mean that social policy has passed, or is passing, out of the realm of controversy. A leading French authority, sur- veying recent developments in his country, used the phrase 'the end of ideologies' as one of his sub-titles and said that it was no longer social policy as such that was in question, but only the modalities of its execution.[9] But this, perhaps, overestimates the extent to which the processes of integration we have described have as yet produced a unitary policy that is clear and consistent. They have managed, as it were, to bring all the various pieces of machinery together in the same workshop, and to make a list of the jobs they have to do. But that is not quite the end of the matter. The German writer, Gerhard Mackenroth, said that the task of social policy was to determine the order of priority of claims against the national product.[10] A policy that reached that point would have carried integration to its ultimate limit. And it may well be that this gives us the clue to the events of the next few decades.

1   Margaret Wynn, *Fatherless Families*, p. 45
2   W. Haber and W. J. Cohen, *Readings in Social Security*, p. 54
3   Beveridge Report, title of 'Change 2' on p. 22
4   A. T. Peacock and J. Wiseman, *The Growth of Public Expenditure in the UK*, p. 86, supplemented from the Tables on pp. 114 and 119 in A. T. Peacock and D. J. Robertson (ed.), *Public Expenditure—Appraisal and Control*
5   ILO, *The Cost of Social Security*, 1949–57, p. 205
6   Arthur P. Miles, *American Social Work Theory*, p. 6
7   F. Zweig, *The Worker in an Affluent Society*, p. 212
8   B. Abel-Smith, 'Whose Welfare State?' in Norman Mackenzie (ed.), *Conviction*, p. 57
9   Jean-Daniel Reynaud, 'La sécurité sociale en France' in *European Journal of Sociology*, 1961, no. 2, pp. 270–2
10 Erik Boettcher (ed.), *Sozialpolitik und Sozialreform*, p. 49

Select bibliography

Most of the titles in this list appear also in the bibliographical notes attached to each chapter. They have been selected with a view to giving a wide variety of sources in a small compass. Acts of Parliament and Annual Reports of Ministries are not included.

I GENERAL

Archer, Peter (ed.), *Social Welfare and the Citizen* (Pelican), 1957
Bruce, Maurice, *The Coming of the Welfare State*, 1961
Fabian Essays (Jubilee edition), 1948
Fogarty, Michael P., *Under-governed and Over-governed*, 1962
Hall, M. Penelope, *The Social Services of Modern England* (5th ed.), 1960
Macleod, Iain and Powell, J. Enoch, *The Social Services—Needs and Means*, 1958
Marshall, T. H., *Sociology at the Crossroads*, Part III, 1963
Robson, W. A., *The Welfare State* in Hobhouse Memorial Lectures, 1951–60
Titmuss, R. M., *Essays on the Welfare State*, 1958

II SOCIAL SECURITY

(a) *General*

Beveridge, W. H. (Lord), *Insurance for All and Everything*, 1924
Beveridge, W. H. (Lord), *Social Insurance and Allied Services* (*The Beveridge Report*), 1942
Burns, Eveline M., *The American Social Security System*, 1951
Dawson, W. H., *Social Insurance in Germany*, 1912
European Economic Community, *Série Politique Sociale*, No. 3, 1962
Laroque, Pierre, 'From Social Insurance to Social Security' (*International Labour Review*, 1948)
Marsh, David C., *National Insurance and Assistance in Great Britain*, 1950

Robson, W. A. (ed.), *Social Security* (2nd ed.), 1945
Williams, Gertrude, *The State and the Standard of Living*, 1936

(b) *Pensions*
Abel-Smith, Brian and Townsend, P., *New Pensions for Old* (Fabian Research Series, No. 171), 1955
Cole, Dorothy, *The Economic Circumstances of Old People*, 1962
'Germany's New Pension Scheme', *Industry and Labour*, 1957
Michanek, Ernst, *Sweden's New National Pension Insurance*, 1960
Pilch, M. and Wood, V., *Pension Schemes*, 1960
Sutherland, William, *Old Age Pensions in Theory and Practice*, 1907
White Paper on 'Provision for Old Age', 1958
Wilson, Sir Arnold and Mackay, G. S., *Old Age Pensions*, 1941

(c) *Unemployment and Industrial Injury*
Beveridge, W. H. (Lord), *The Past and Present of Unemployment Insurance*, 1930
Cheit, Earl F. and Gordon, Margaret S. (ed.), *Occupational Disability and Public Policy*, 1964
Davison, Ronald C., *British Unemployment Policy since 1930*, 1938
Tillyard, Sir Frank and Ball, F. N., *Unemployment Insurance in Great Britain, 1911–48*, 1949
                Note. For Health Insurance see 'Health'

III   POVERTY AND ITS RELIEF

Lynes, Tony, *National Assistance and National Prosperity*, 1962
P.E.P., *Poverty Ten years after Beveridge* (*Planning*, No. 344), 1952
Rowntree, B. S. and Lavers, G. R., *Poverty and the Welfare State*, 1951
Royal Commission on the Poor Laws and Relief of Distress, 1905–9 (Parliamentry Papers 1909, Vol. XXXVII).
Webb, Sidney and Beatrice, *English Poor Law History*, Part II, Vol. 2
Wedderburn, D. Cole, 'Poverty in Britain Today' (*Sociological Review*, 1962)

IV   SOCIAL WELFARE

Curtis Committee, Report on the Care of Children, Cmd. 6922, 1946
Donnison, D. V., *The Neglected Child and the Social Services*, 1954

Ford, Donald, *The Delinquent Child and the Community*, 1957

Heywood, Jean S., *Children in Care*, 1959

Marris, Peter, *Widows and their Families*, 1958

Philp, A. F. and Timms, N., *The Problem of the 'Problem Family'*, 1957

Rodgers, Barbara and Dixon, Julia, *Portrait of Social Work*, 1960

Ruck, S. K., *London Government and the Welfare Services*, 1963

Shenfield, B. E., *Social Policies for Old Age*, 1957

Townsend, Peter, *The Last Refuge*, 1962

Wynn, Margaret, *Fatherless Families*, 1964

Younghusband Report on Social Workers in the Local Authority Health and Welfare Services, 1959

V HEALTH

Eckstein, Harry, *The English Health Service*, 1959

Farndale, W. A. J. (ed.), *Trends in the National Health Service*, 1964

Gillie Report on the Field of Work of the Family Doctor, 1963

Harris, R. W., *National Health Insurance in Great Britain, 1911–46*, 1946

Jones, Kathleen, *Mental Health and Social Policy, 1845–1959*, 1960

Lindsey, Almont, *Socialized Medicine in England and Wales*, 1962

Mackintosh, J. M., *Trends of Opinion about the Public Health, 1901–51*, 1953

Porritt Report—Review of the Medical Services in Great Britain, 1962

Serbein, Oscar, *Paying for Medical Care in the United States*, 1953

Taylor, Stephen (Lord), *Good General Practice*, 1954

World Health Organization, First and Second Reports on the World Health Situation, 1959 and 1962

VI HOUSING

Bowley, Marian, *Housing and the State, 1919–44*, 1945

Cullingworth, J. B., *Housing Needs and Planning Policy*, 1960

Donnison, D. V. et al., *Housing since the Rent Act*, 1962

Greve, John, *The Housing Problem* (Fabian Research Series, No. 224), 1961

Wendt, Paul F., *Housing Policy, the Search for Solutions*, 1962

VII FINANCE

Abel-Smith, Brian, *Paying for Health Services* (W.H.O. Public Health Papers, No. 17), 1963
Abel-Smith, Brian and Titmuss, R. M., *The Cost of the National Health Service*, 1956
International Labour Organization, *The Cost of Social Security, 1949–57*, 1961
Peacock, A. T. (ed.), *Income Redistribution and Social Policy*, 1954
Peacock, A. T. and Wiseman, J., *The Growth of Public Expenditure in the U.K.*, 1961
Richardson, J. Henry, *Economic and Financial Aspects of Social Security*, 1960

VIII VOLUNTARY ORGANIZATIONS

Beveridge, Lord, *Voluntary Action*, 1948
Bourdillon, A. F. C. (ed.), *Voluntary Social Services*, 1945
Mowat, C. L., *The Charity Organization Society, 1869–1913*, 1961
Rooff, Madeline, *Voluntary Societies and Social Policy*, 1957
Woodroofe, Kathleen, *From Charity to Social Work in England and the United States,* 1962

NOTE ON PERIODICAL PUBLICATIONS

Articles on social policy appear in many journals. The following are particularly useful as sources of factual information:

Bulletin of the International Social Security Association (*1948–*)
European Economic Community. Annual Reports on the Social Situation (1958–)
International Labour Organization, *Industry and Labour* (1949–61)
International Labour Review (1921–)
New Society (October 1962–)

Index